How to use E

In this issue

The 92 daily readings in this issue of *Explore* are designed to help you understand and apply the Bible as you read it each day.

It's serious!

We suggest that you allow 15 minutes each day to work through the Bible passage with the notes. It should be a meal, not a snack! Readings from other parts of the Bible can throw valuable light on the study passage. These cross-references can be skipped if you are already feeling full up, but will expand your grasp of the Bible. *Explore* uses the NIV2011 Bible translation, but you can also use it with the NIV1984 or ESV translations.

Sometimes a prayer section will encourage you to stop and pray through the lessons—but it is always important to allow time to pray for God's Spirit to bring his word to life, and to shape the way we think and live through it.

We're serious!

All of us who work on *Explore* share a passion for getting the Bible into people's lives. We fiercely hold to the Bible as God's word— to honour and follow, not to explain away.

1 Find a time you can read the Bible each day

2 Find a place where you can be quiet and think

3 Ask God to help you understand

4 Carefully read through the Bible passage for today

5 Study the verses with Explore, taking time to think

6 Pray about what you have read

Welcome to the 100th Issue of Explore

Tim Thornborough is the Publishing Director
at The Good Book Company

It's good to celebrate milestones. And this issue of *Explore* is a significant one. Several of our regular writers, and a couple of guest contributors, have given us something new and different to encourage and help us in this special issue.

On the whole, *Explore* works through books of the Bible. This sometimes means that we are reading long passages of scripture to get the grand sweep of the story and its message. But there's also great value in slowing down and considering the detail.

So for this issue, I asked a group of trusted teachers a simple question: *What's your favourite verse in the Bible?* And then asked them to write a week's worth of notes taking us by the hand through the text word by word. So in addition to some regular book-length sections, we'll also be spending time digging deep into single verses chosen, among others, by Sinclair Ferguson, Marcus Nodder and Tim Chester. I hope you find that this brings a freshness to your daily Bible reading as we close off 2022. Let us know, either by email or through the *Explore* Facebook page, what you think of this experiment, and whether you think it's a helpful feature that we could continue as we go on towards issue 200.

My grateful thanks to the many people who labour to make *Explore* the discipleship resource that it is. Most of the writers are working pastors who long to bring the insight and refreshment of God's word to ordinary Christians. The thoughts they share on the page have often come from their regular preaching, and I am grateful for the effort they put in to enrich others.

My thanks as well to those at The Good Book Company who, over the years have worked to make *Explore* as excellent as possible. Alison Mitchell, Caroline Napper and Anne Woodcock and have all improved *Explore* in unique ways as they have worked at the proofs and offered further insights. Editorial Director Carl Laferton is the iron that sharpens iron for the whole output of The Good Book Company, and his constant encouragement keeps us all striving for higher standards.

And a special thanks to God for Phil Crowter—now in glory—who first started *Explore* more than 25 years ago as a way of encouraging believers. Phil's vision to confidently proclaim and lovingly apply God's word is a vision we enthusiastically share, and we are grateful to God for the selfless way he entrusted this resource to us, and was such an encouragement to us in our early years.

But most of all we thank God for you, our readers. Our aim at The Good Book Company is to serve the church, and the ordinary believers who make up the glorious company of the saints. Thank you for your support, feedback, encouragement and questions. Let's keep digging daily into God's word together so that we can serve him who gave his life for us, and is taking us to eternity.

LUKE: Who are the guests?

Jesus has healed a man during a banquet (v 1-6)—a glimpse, perhaps, of the banquet in God's kingdom (Isaiah 25:6-9). What a blessing it will be to sit at that table!

RSVP

Read Luke 14:15-21

Planning a party in the first century required that a servant be sent out to extend invitations and return with a sense of who would be coming. Plans could then proceed with certainty about the number of people who had agreed to come. Once all was prepared, a servant was dispatched to call the guests to come to the feast (v 17). Obviously, in those days (as in ours!) to back out of the invitation at this point was very rude.

> ❷ *How does this help us to feel the shock of verses 18-20?*
> ❷ *How does this help explain the reaction of the master in verse 21?*

Jesus wants his hearers to draw a straight line from the parable to the Pharisees crowded around him at this dinner party. In the person of Jesus, God was extending invitations to the end-time messianic banquet, and it would surely be the strict and religious Pharisees who were at the top of the guest list. But they had responded to the invitation with rudeness and opposition, and so now the indignant host was prepared to act in an equally shocking way.

Revised guest list

Read Luke 14:22-24

> ❷ *What is the master determined to ensure happens?*

❷ *Who ends up at the banquet?*

These people could not lend any prestige to the gathering—their only qualification for attendance was their willingness to accept the invitation.

Make sure you see both the invitation and the warning for us. The people who we'd expect to be at the party—the religious, the wealthy, the successful—these are the ones who find themselves excluded, because they have excluded themselves. We are all given a chance to respond to Jesus' kingdom invitation, but we should not presume that our invitation is permanent or our acceptance is automatic. If we make other things—work, family, anything—a priority above coming to the feast of the kingdom, we will find that we are shut out. The only ones who end up at the banquet are those who know they don't deserve to be there, and who gratefully accept the invitation—those who are humble (v 11).

⌃ Pray

While all our hearts and all our songs
Join to admire the feast,
Each of us cry, with thankful tongues,
"Lord, why was I a guest?"
(Issac Watts, "How Sweet and Aweful is the Place")

Let these words be the basis of your prayers of grateful, humble thanks today.

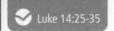

Finish what you start

It's easy to think that evangelism is about making following Jesus seem as easy and painless as possible. In which case, Jesus made a terrible evangelist…

Cross-carriers required

Read Luke 14:25-27

❓ *How popular is Jesus (v 25)?*
❓ *What does he say in response about what following him must involve?*
 •*v 26*   •*v 27*

In Jesus' day, "hate" could mean the thing that was rejected in a choice between two important possibilities. It is best to take Jesus' words in verse 26 in terms of priority; Jesus must have our absolute loyalty and commitment. But understanding this does not make verse 26 any less challenging.

A tower and a war

Read Luke 14:28-35

❓ *If you are building a tower, what would you do before you start, and why (v 28-30)?*
❓ *If you are a king considering going to war, what would you do before you start, and why (v 31-32)?*

The question in each case is: *do you have the resources and strength required to bear the cost of what you are doing, and so to finish what you are starting?*

Jesus makes it clear that being his disciple will cost a person everything that they have (v 33). He requires every person to renounce one hundred percent of what they have, whether that be very little or very much. The point is not that all give up the same

things to follow Jesus, but rather, that all must be willing to give up everything they have if Jesus requires it. There is nothing in a disciple's life that is off-limits to Jesus; following him means you have no powers of veto when it comes to his plans for you. If following him requires us to give up financial security, creature comforts, good schools for our kids, the respect of others, or even our long-cherished hopes and plans for our lives, then so be it.

❓ *Why do you think Jesus wants the crowds to understand this?*
❓ *Would it have been better or worse for him to have kept quiet and not risked the crowds melting away?*

⌄ Apply

❓ *How does Jesus' view of discipleship differ from your own version of it?*
❓ *In which areas are you most tempted to make something or someone else a priority, or to compromise on carrying your cross?*
❓ *Does your message in evangelism need to change? How?*

⌃ Pray

Read Luke 18:29-30 and Philippians 1:6.
Thank Jesus that while following him costs you everything you have, it also gives you everything you need. Pray that you will have grace to finish the life you have started.

Bible in a year: Ezekiel 30-32 • John 15

Who does God love?

What kind of person does God love? Our culture tends to assume that it's everybody—apart from, possibly, terrorists and murderers.

But once we say "apart from", we start to get a little close to home. How should God feel about unfaithful husbands? Mothers who lose their tempers and hit their children in anger? Tax cheats? Those with anger issues? Proud, hurtful, selfish people?

The three parables that Luke records in chapter 15 go a long way towards providing Jesus' answer to the question: *what kind of person does God love?*

Two groups

Read Luke 15:1-2

❓ *Who wanted to hear Jesus (v 1)?*
❓ *Who did this offend, and why (v 2)?*

It is not just that Jesus is tolerating the unworthy. He is welcoming them. So having challenged the keen crowds with the cost of discipleship (14:25-33), Jesus now challenges the proud Pharisees with the depth of God's mercy for the lost.

Two stories

Read Luke 15:1-10

❓ *Why would it, in many ways, have made more sense for this shepherd to write off the loss of a single sheep?*
❓ *What is the happy ending of the story (v 5-6)?*
❓ *The "coin" (v 8) was worth a day's wages. How would you feel if you lost that amount?*

❓ *What are the two parables meant to tell us about God?*

The two little stories that Jesus tells are so vivid and engaging that it is easy to miss the larger point. Neither the lost sheep nor the lost coin is the main character in their parable; the centre of each story is the passionate search that is undertaken in order to find the lost item. What is the love of God like? It is like a shepherd who would go to extremes —leaving his flock, travelling all over the wilderness, and carrying a hundred-pound (45 kg) animal on his shoulders—in order to see his lost sheep restored. It is like the sick-to-her-stomach sensation a woman would feel if she discovered that 10% of her personal wealth had gone missing; nothing would be right until the coin was found.

That explains Jesus' ministry. He *is* the heavenly search party. Just as the shepherd and the woman spared no effort in order to experience the joy of finding what was lost, so Jesus endured the pain and humiliation of the cross for the joy of seeing lost people restored to God (see Hebrews 12:2).

▾ Apply

❓ *Do you struggle to believe that God loves you? How do these parables reassure you?*
❓ *Do you struggle to remember that you do not earn God's love? How does the parable of the lost sheep humble you?*

Father and sons

Next comes another of Jesus' most famous parables. Each of the three people in it behaves in ways that teach us something important about the dynamic back in v 1-2.

Read Luke 15:1-2, 11-32

The younger son

By asking for his inheritance while his father is alive, this son is saying that he wants to relate to his father now in the way he normally would once his father is dead; he wants to skip ahead to when he can have his father's money without having a father.

- ❓ *How do things work out for him at first (v 13)—and then after that (v 14-16)?*
- ❓ *When "he comes to himself" (the literal translation of v 17), what does he decide to ask his father for?*

The father

- ❓ *Does the father give his son what he is hoping for (compare v 19 and v 22-24)?*
- ❓ *How did the father feel about his wandering son, who had wished him dead (v 20)?*

If you are familiar with this story, it can be hard to appreciate how unexpected this response was. The younger son's behaviour was truly scandalous. The father could not have been blamed if he'd responded to his son's return with suspicion and distance; instead his love was lavish and unrestrained.

The older brother

- ❓ *How does Jesus contrast the two sons' behaviour (compare v 12-13 and v 25a)?*

- ❓ *Do you think the older son's reaction to his brother's welcome in verses 28-30 is justifiable?*
- ❓ *How does the father treat this son compassionately and patiently (v 31-32)?*

Remember, the house is the father's, and the robe, ring, sandals and calf are the father's. Who is the older brother to tell him what to do with these things?! It turns out the son who believed his obedience merited reward from his father was just as lost as the son who believed instant reward lay in disobeying his father.

The question for us is whether we love the same things that our heavenly Father loves. Followers of Jesus should be marked by a compassionate tenderness towards people who are in rebellion against God. We should be running to them, telling them they can enjoy life as a child of God, even after everything. And when a sinner repents and "comes home" through faith in Christ, we ought to be filled with delight that our God is a merciful Father who forgives and restores the lost—including us.

☑ Apply

- ❓ *Are there ways in which you resemble the older brother?*
- ❓ *How grateful are you for your own rescue? How should this show itself in your prayers and your life?*

Financial investments

If Luke 15 contains some of Jesus' most famous and accessible parables, chapter 16 contains some of the most obscure and confusing.

This next one is not hard to understand—but its application can seem puzzling.

Shrewd

Read Luke 16:1-9

❷ *What is the point of the parable, according to Jesus (v 9)?*
❷ *In the parable, what is the manager's problem (v 1-3)?*
❷ *What is his aim (v 4)?*
❷ *How does he achieve his aim (v 5-7)?*

The master's approval (v 8) for his dishonest manager's conduct is surprising! Many explanations have been put forward, but we are probably best simply to be content with Jesus' explanation for the master's positive reaction: "The people of this world are more shrewd in dealing with their own kind than are the people of the light". The master's approval is not a reward for dishonesty, but a tip of the hat to the servant's shrewdness. In terms of sheer self-preservation, this scoundrel cannot be outfoxed; he went to great lengths to secure his own interests.

At the end of verse 8, Jesus drives home his point: the people who belong to the world and share its values know how to get what they want from others through clever planning and activity. God's children, however, sometimes fail to see how they can shrewdly use the things of this world to their spiritual advantage. The dishonest steward behaves wisely according to the world's standards

and the world's values. Similarly, Jesus wants his people to behave wisely according to the standards and values of his kingdom.

So, Jesus says, *use your money and opportunities now in a way that accrues benefit for yourself in heaven.* Again, various explanations have been put forward for the nature of being "welcomed into eternal dwellings"—perhaps it is the welcome of those who have gone there before us, who our "investments" helped bring into the kingdom (e.g. the work of the missionary we helped fund, the children's group we helped lead, etc.).

Trustworthy

Read Luke 16:10-12

❷ *What do you think it means to be "trustworthy" in handling the worldly wealth our Father has chosen to give us?*
❷ *If we see our money as "someone else's property", how will that change our use of it, do you think (v 12)?*

The way we handle our worldly wealth (something of relatively little eternal importance) is a matter of eternal significance.

✔ Apply

❷ *Think about your own spending, saving and giving. Does it show that you are investing your wealth with eternal considerations in mind? Does anything need to change?*

Jesus, money and law

In the end, our relationship to money is one of love and service. We either use it to serve the one we love, or we serve it because it is the one we love.

One master only

Read Luke 16:13-15

❓ *Who fell into this category of money-lovers (v 14)?*
❓ *What is the huge spiritual danger of living like this (v 13)?*
❓ *In what different ways is it possible to worship money as a god?*

Our finances are an important means by which we can worship God. We can pay lip service to generosity to the things of God, but the one who sees our hearts (v 15) knows whether we truly love him, or our money. God is after our hearts and our love.

⌃ Pray

Consider some of the ways the living God is a better master than money (there are many!). Then ask God to help you to see your heart rightly, and to see any ways in which you are serving a master other than him. Ask for grace to understand what it would mean to serve him and love him in that area, and for strength to change.

How to view the law

Verses 13-15 have begun to shift the focus of Jesus' teaching from his disciples (v 1) to the Pharisees, those lovers of money (v 14). They objected to everything about Jesus' ministry, including his approach to God's law (see 14:1-6).

Read Luke 16:16-18

❓ *In what sense have things changed now Jesus has come (v 16)?*
❓ *How have things not changed (v 17)?*

Jesus understood that his arrival signified the fulfilment of the law (Matthew 5:17-18). Far from nullifying the law, Jesus was bringing it to its ultimate purpose. He was fulfilling the promise and meaning of the Old Testament in his life, his teaching and his substitutionary death and resurrection.

So if Christ fulfils the law—if it all points to him, and he has now come—does God no longer care about his people's holiness?

❓ *How does Luke 16:18 answer that question?*

This goes beyond the letter of OT law. Jesus presses on his followers the expectation that they will seek in this sense to go beyond the law and comply with God's original intent for marriage. The arrival of the kingdom does not nullify the law, but transforms the hearts of its citizens so that they will long to obey God's will (see Jeremiah 31:33).

⌄ Apply

❓ *In what ways are you...*
  • *ignoring God's law?*
  • *doing the bare minimum by just obeying the letter of the law?*
  • *seeking to please God by aligning your heart and life with his intentions?*

Can't take it with you

Jesus now tells another parable to press home the great spiritual danger of loving money. It is one that we, in our materialist culture, need to hear.

This life
Read Luke 16:19-23

❓ *What are the contrasts between the two main characters in verses 19-21?*

The fact that Lazarus "was laid" (literally "was thrown") outside the gate and was unable to prevent the indignity of having his sores licked by wild dogs seems to indicate that he was in some way an invalid.

In a world with no organised social-relief programmes, people in Lazarus' position were dependent on the generosity of people like the rich man (a generosity on which the Old Testament law insisted—see Deuteronomy 15:7-8 for one example). The rich man was clearly aware of Lazarus' presence at his gate and his extreme need, for he knew the beggar's name without being told (see Luke 16:24). But there is no indication that he ever did anything to address the poor man's longing and suffering.

❓ *How are things reversed in eternity (v 22-23)?*

The next life
Read Luke 16:24-26

❓ *What do these verses teach us about the nature of Hades (hell)?*

When the ex-rich man appeals to Abraham as his spiritual father (v 24, 27), his request meets the same fate as that of so many of Lazarus' pleas during the earthly life of the two men. Abraham might formally call him "son" (v 25), but the rich man never acted much like a son of Abraham by keeping the law during his life, and so now in death he finds himself quite alone.

❓ *How is Jesus pressing home the spiritual danger of loving money?*

All they need
Read Luke 16:27-31

❓ *What two requests does the rich man make (v 27-28, 30)?*
❓ *Why will neither plan work (v 29, 31)?*

When we fail to trust and worship God, the problem is not that we do not have enough reason to do so. We have both Moses and the Prophets, and also the words of a man who rose from the dead. We are not lacking instruction about how we ought to think about money and riches. The only question is whether we are listening.

☑ Apply

Again, this parable invites us to examine our view of our money and possessions.

❓ *Does your generosity towards those in need reflect a heart that loves God? Or is your heart so fixed on enjoying wealth and comfort that you are receiving all your good things in this life (v 25)?*
❓ *How will you live and spend with eternity in mind today?*

Bible in a year: Ezekiel 42-44 • John 19:1-22

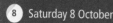

Now but not yet

The key to understanding the overarching theme of chapters 17 – 18 of Luke lies in the Pharisees' question in 17:20, and the start of Jesus' answer to it in v 21-22.

It is in your midst

Read Luke 17:20-22

❓ *What are the Pharisees asking (v 20)?*
❓ *But what can't you do, according to Jesus (v 20)? Why not (v 21)?*

The Pharisees are looking for signs that the kingdom is coming that are observable in the physical world. But the kingdom is "within you"—or better, "in your midst". The kingdom is present right then, because the King is present among them. But equally, Jesus tells his disciples that they will long to see "one of the days of the Son of Man"—a reference to Jesus' return to Earth in splendour to judge God's enemies and vindicate his people.

In other words, Jesus' kingdom is both now and not yet—it came when Christ came, but has not yet come in all its glorious fullness. We are part of the kingdom, but we are waiting for the kingdom. And these two chapters will show us what it looks like to live in this time of now-but-not-yet.

How to live right now

Read Luke 17:1-10

❓ *Though temptations are "bound to come", what must we be ruthless about (v 1-3a)?*
❓ *Given that sin in this time is going to be a reality, how must we treat one another (v 3b-4)?*

❓ *What size faith is necessary to get on with obeying Jesus in the ways he's just set out (v 6)?*
❓ *How is this both encouraging for us and challenging to us?*
❓ *When we do obey Jesus, perhaps in one of the ways he details in verses 1-4, what should our attitude to that obedience be (v 10)? Why (v 7-9)?*

Humility is key to living as Christians. The fact is that God is incredibly kind and gracious to his servants, but that love and care is rooted in his character, not in our performance. When we fail to obey him, we find our master forgiving us. When we do obey, we have only done what we should do as faithful servants. That humble attitude gives glory to God, where it belongs.

Likewise, faith is key to living in this now-but-not-yet time. Faith looks back to Jesus and sees the way that all of God's promises have already become a "Yes" for us in him (2 Corinthians 1:20). Faith also looks forward to the return of the Son of Man as the day when all of the promises of God will be fulfilled completely. Faith grabs hold both of what God has done and what he said he will do, and lives accordingly.

☑ Apply

❓ *How will you live humbly, and by faith, today? What problems, challenges or temptations might stop you?*

An ever-present help

How do you respond to trouble? Do you worry about it, deny it, or try to fix it?

The Israelites were in trouble—surrounded by warring nations, many of which would have loved to wipe them off the map. How would they cope with this constant threat to national security?

No fear
Read Psalm 46:1-3

❷ *Why are the Israelites not afraid, although humanly speaking they should be (v 1)?*

❷ *How would remembering these truths about God help them in their trouble?*

❷ *What picture does the psalmist conjure up in verses 2-3? What would it feel like to experience this?*

By using images of natural disasters, the psalmist helps us to visualise the terrifying situation the Israelites have found themselves in.

Know God
Read Psalm 46:4-7

The scene shifts to Jerusalem, which was vulnerable to attack and besiegement.

❷ *What is the contrast between the water of verses 2-3 and the water of verse 4?*

❷ *What contrast is made between the mountains and the city of God (v 2, 5)?*

❷ *How would this section encourage God's people?*

These verses are like balm on a wound. God's city is completely secure—an oasis of joy and peace in the midst of chaos— because he is dwelling within her.

❷ *How does this apply to us? (Hint: read Ephesians 2:19-22.)*

Be still
Read Psalm 46:8-11

❷ *What does God do in verses 8-9?*

❷ *What does this teach us about him?*

❷ *Who is God addressing in verse 10?*

❷ *Why is it pointless to oppose God?*

❷ *Why do you think the psalmist repeats verse 7 in verse 11?*

We might read verse 10 as a gentle encouragement to rest in God's sovereignty—but it's actually a stern command to the nations, calling them to submit themselves to God before it's too late. He is the awesome Lord of history, the one who controls all armies, governments, bosses and families. And that's why we, as his people, have no need to fear anything at all.

☑ Apply
Re-read Psalm 46:1

❷ *Why does knowing that God is for you give you peace in troubled times?*

❷ *How will this psalm help you to turn to God at the first sight of trouble?*

Thank you

Today's is a short study, to allow you a lot of time to apply its teaching straight away!

....

Healed, restored...

Read Luke 17:11-19

Leprosy was a terrible disease, and those who were afflicted with it were required to stand at a distance (v 12) lest they infect healthy people.

❓ *What does Jesus do for them (v 13-14)?*
❓ *What does Jesus find surprising about the response of the lepers (v 15-18)?*

"Made you well" (v 19) can also be translated "saved you". That makes sense of verse 19—after all, this man has already been healed of his leprosy, and so were the other nine who showed no grateful faith. Verse 19 suggests that this man's gratitude displays his faith: a faith that reaches out to Jesus not only for healing but also for saving.

If the message of the gospel of the kingdom is that Jesus' followers have been cleansed from a far more terrible pollution (sin), then how much more should they be overwhelmed by gratitude? If you are a Christian, you should live lives of genuine gratitude to God for what you have received. Whatever else your day involves, it should include time spent thanking God for the mercy he has had on you.

... forgiven

🔼 Pray

Spend time now praising God, throwing yourself at Jesus' feet and thanking him for what he has rescued you from, and rescued you for. You might find it helpful to use these passages to fuel your gratitude: **Ephesians 1:3-14; 1 Peter 1:3-6; Isaiah 52:13 – 53:12.**

Like the lightning

Where is this world headed? Might we miss Jesus' return? What will happen when he comes?

Read Luke 17:22-37

You won't miss it

- ❷ *How should Jesus' followers react to claims of Jesus' return (v 23)?*
- ❷ *Why do we not need to wonder whether or not he has come (v 24)?*

It will be an event that is not easily missed or misunderstood; this seems to be the meaning of the curious expression in v 37. When asked where these things will happen, Jesus replied, "Where there is a dead body, there the vultures will gather". That is to say, it is easy to locate a corpse when you see vultures swarming around it. In the same way, the events surrounding Jesus' return will not be difficult to see. No one will miss it. He might have been rejected by the generation who saw him when he lived on Earth (v 25), but he will be recognised by everyone when he returns in all his power.

☑ Apply

Next time you see lightning, remember: God created lightning to give us a visual illustration of what Jesus' return will be like.

You must be ready for it

- ❷ *What are the similarities between the coming of the flood, the coming of destruction on Sodom and Gomorrah, and the coming of the Lord (v 26-30)?*

- ❷ *How does v 27 help us when the return of the Lord Jesus feels unlikely to us?*

There will be no opportunity to make preparations once that day has arrived (v 31); they must not fail to obey the Lord's instructions as Lot's wife did (v 32—see Genesis 19:26). In light of that reality, Jesus repeats his call to discipleship in Luke 17:33: "Whoever tries to keep their life will lose it, and whoever loses their life will preserve it".

☑ Apply

Read Revelation 1:12-18; 19:6-9; 21:1-5

- ❷ *How do these verses make you feel about the return of the Lord Jesus?*
- ❷ *Are you looking forward to Jesus' return more than you are looking forward to anything else in your life? Is there any danger that if he returned today, you would, like Lot's wife, regret what you leave behind or have not experienced in this life?*

◮ Pray

Lord Jesus, thank you for facing suffering and rejection in order to save me. Thank you that you will return to reign—and that your kingdom includes me. Help me to live each day as though it may be the day you return. Help me to face the ups, downs, hopes and dreams of this life with my eyes fixed on the day when you come back. Amen.

Bible in a year: Song of Songs 4-5 • Ephesians 1 ✔

A widow and a judge

What should we do while we wait for the day of Jesus' return? This parable has a very simple lesson: pray, and don't give up (18:1).

The characters

Read Luke 18:1-5

❓ *What type of person is the widow?*

❓ *What type of person is the judge?*

❓ *What does the widow need and how does she get it (v 3-5)?*

The truth

Read Luke 18:6-8

If we are surprised by the judge's cynicism and selfishness, we must be shocked when Jesus ("the Lord") instructs his followers to listen to the judge (v 6). What possible lesson could we be meant to learn from this man? Jesus here argues from the lesser to the greater: if this lazy and indifferent judge can be prevailed upon by persistent petition, how much more will God "bring about justice for his chosen ones, who cry out to him day and night?" (v 7) The point is that God is much better than the unjust judge, and so if the judge secures justice for the widow, we can be certain that our heavenly Father will make sure that those who cry out to him get justice, and quickly (v 8).

The widow never gave up her faith that the judge would grant her justice. That is why she kept on asking...

❓ *What is Jesus' challenge to us (v 8)?*

In context, this parable is not about persistence in prayer generally (though that is a

good thing!), for Jesus concludes the lesson with this question about his return: will the Son of Man find faith when he comes? Luke's comment in verse 1 is specifically referring to prayer regarding the return of Jesus. We have been warned about the danger of going about daily life unaware of Christ's imminent return (17:26-35). Instead, disciples should long to see that day (17:22) and so persist in steadfast prayer for Jesus' return and all the justice he will bring to the world and for his people.

⌄ Apply

❓ *What happens to our view of our world, our lives and the suffering of those we love if we forget that God will "bring about justice for his chosen ones"?*

❓ *How often do you pray along these lines? How might you build it into your daily prayers?*

❓ *Is there something specific you need to "cry out" to God about, rather than bottling it up or giving up hope about it?*

⌃ Pray

Pray, and don't give up!

A good man and a sinner

The King has come, and the kingdom is coming in fullness when he returns. But—who is part of that kingdom? What is the entry requirement?

Two men

Read Luke 18:9-10

The Pharisees were widely respected for their piety and devotion to the Torah, and this particular man's religious rigour (as described in v 12, and we have no reason to doubt his truthfulness) exceeded that which God required of his people in the Law of Moses. Tax collectors in Judea, on the other hand, were widely despised as traitors, thieves and oppressors of their own people. We need to hear the next verses in the same way Jesus' first listeners would have done—or we will miss the shock, and the challenge.

Two approaches

Read Luke 18:11-13

> ❷ On what basis does the Pharisee approach God (v 11-12)?

This is justification-by-good-works—if I keep the religious rules well enough, I will merit blessing. It produces pride and judgmentalism because what counts is how hard you work, how well you do, and how much better you are than others.

> ❷ In what way and on what basis does the tax collector approach God (v 13)?

Ironically, it's the tax collector who has remembered the whole purpose of the building in which they stand. The temple was the place where God showed his commitment to be merciful to sinners through the sacrificial system—where he graciously told his people an animal could die in their place, for their sin. The Pharisee is too busy thinking about his goodness to consider his need for God's forgiveness!

Two verdicts

Read Luke 18:14

> ❷ Which one of the two men does Jesus say is right with God (justified)?

Jesus is destroying the fundamental principle of virtually every religion! The pride and self-exaltation that would dare to hold up our own goodness as reason for God's love will lead to a terrible humbling, but "those who humble themselves will be exalted".

☑ Apply

Christians are not immune from the attitude of the Pharisee.

> ❷ On what basis do you expect God to bless you, or not to bless you? Do you consider yourself more deserving of his blessing than a murderer or conman?
> ❷ Do you think that you bring anything to your salvation other than your sin and your cry for mercy?

☖ Pray

God, have mercy on me, a sinner. Amen.

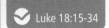

The kids and the ruler

Now we see the story of the parable of the Pharisee and the tax collector worked out in real life.

They come
Read Luke 18:15-17

Modern Western societies tend to idealise childhood as a time of innocence, but this view was unknown in Jesus' day. Children were right next to tax collectors in terms of people with whom an important rabbi would never think to concern himself. In the first century, the disciples' reaction in verse 15 would sound very reasonable.

> ❷ *How is Jesus different (v 16)?*
> ❷ *What is the lesson for adults (v 17)?*

Don't interpret Jesus' words too romantically. He is not saying children are so innocent and lovely that they are worthy of the kingdom of God: quite the opposite. The qualities that children possess are unworthiness and neediness; like the tax collector, they have no resumé of spiritual accomplishments to tempt them to the works-righteousness that marked the Pharisee.

He runs
Read Luke 18:18-25

> ❷ *What does the "ruler" have going for him, spiritually speaking (v 21)?*

He is also "very wealthy" (v 23), which would have been seen as a sign of blessing.

> ❷ *But despite his wealth and his law-keeping, what does he still appear to be anxious about (v 18)?*

Jesus' response in verse 19 is not to deny his own divinity, but to point this man to the only standard of "good'" that counts—the holiness of God. *Can you attain to this standard?* Jesus is implicitly asking.

> ❷ *What is the answer to the man's question in verse 18, does Jesus say (v 22)?*

Jesus is focusing on the thing this man loves very much: his money. And he is saying, *Make me first in your heart, and I will be your King, and you will have great treasure in my kingdom.* But this ruler won't do that; he loves his earthly treasures too much.

Possible impossibility
Read Luke 18:26-34

> ❷ *How is verse 27 a summary of what we've learned through looking at the Pharisee and the rich ruler?*
> ❷ *How do verses 31-34 indicate how it is possible for a tax collector and a child—and you and me—to be saved?*
> ❷ *How do verses 29-30 point out the tragedy of the rich ruler's decision?*

✓ Apply

> ❷ *What would you most struggle to give up or give away if Jesus called you to? That is the place you will be most tempted to turn your back on his kingdom.*
> ❷ *How do v 29-30 empower us to give up the best of this life to follow Jesus joyfully?*

Sing (joyfully)

What's your take on singing in church? The highlight of your week? An endurance test? An opportunity to plan Sunday lunch? Well, this psalm challenges us all!

Read Psalm 47

The what

❷ *Who is the writer of the psalm speaking to (v 1)?*
❷ *What is he calling them to do (v 1, 6)?*
❷ *What is the mood of the psalm?*

There's a time and a place for quiet, contemplative singing, but that's certainly not what's happening here! They're clapping, shouting and singing at the tops of their voices in exuberant praise. There's no embarrassment—no sideways glances or mumbling into the hymn sheet. All they care about is the one they're singing to!

···· TIME OUT ·····································

❷ *When as a Christian have you felt like clapping your hands and singing for joy?*

The why

We've seen that feelings are important—but most of this psalm is taken up with giving reasons for the feelings. We need to engage our minds with truths about God's character and actions in order to praise him rightly.

❷ *What truths about God are declared in:*
  • v 2, 5, 7, 8? • v 3-4? • v 9?

At the time this psalm was written, people believed that each nation was nurtured by its own "gods". But in contrast to the false gods of the nations, the God of Israel is concerned for all peoples, not just his own. He has made them all, and reigns over them all as their King. That's why he deserves their praise!

But there's something puzzling in verses 3-4, isn't there? Why would the nations be praising God for what he's done for Israel? It's caused them to be defeated in battle and lose territory! The clue is in verse 9. The physical nation of Israel was an integral but temporary part of God's salvation plan for all nations.

Read Galatians 3:7-9

❷ *How do these verses help to explain Psalm 47:9?*

Jesus is the key that unlocks salvation for the whole world. Membership of God's people is open to anyone, and defined purely by faith in Jesus' death.

⌄ Apply

❷ *Who can you prayerfully invite to church, to join in with the singing of the nations?*
❷ *How will the example of these verses change the way you engage your mind as you sing to God?*

⌃ Pray

Read Revelation 21:22-27. Use this wonderful passage to praise our King for his remarkable, inclusive salvation plan.

Bible in a year: 1 Samuel 7-9 • Ephesians 5:1-16 ⌄

City of the great King

This psalm is the flipside of Psalm 46. There, God's people seek to trust him when Jerusalem is under threat. Here, they joyfully praise him after the threat has passed.

Praise
Read Psalm 48:1-3

❷ How is the city described?
❷ What is the connection between God and the city?

"Zaphon" (v 2) is Hebrew for "north", and is used here not geographically, but in the sense of "heaven" or "God's throne". It's his city—he protects it, he promotes it, and therefore he is to be praised for it.

Proof

Now we're given a specific example of how God cares for his city.

Read Psalm 48:4-8

❷ What kind of event is being described?
❷ What effect does the city have on the kings? Why?
❷ What do God's people learn from the experience (v 8)?

It's not much of a fight, is it? These strutting, self-confident armies are utterly floored once they reach the city. It's not clear how exactly they were defeated, but there's no doubt at all over the cause.

···· **TIME OUT** ·································

Jerusalem was defeated by the Babylonians in 586 BC, and destroyed by the Romans in AD 70. How can we square this with v 8?

Read Revelation 21:1-4

❷ How does this help us understand where psalms such as this are pointing?
❷ What other shadows of the new Jerusalem do you see in this psalm?

The earthly Jerusalem was only a fleeting shadow cast by the real city of the great King.

Ponder
Read Psalm 48:9-14

❷ How do God's people respond in:
• v 9? • v 10? • v 11? • v 12-14?
❷ What does this tell us about their heart attitude towards their victory?

There's no bragging, no scramble to claim the credit. Instead, the inhabitants of Zion join together to wonder at the gracious character of God. There's joy in abundance, but also quiet contemplation. They celebrate with a victory lap of their city walls, but it's God they're pointing to all the way round.

Apply

Jesus has won a much greater victory for us at the cross. He has granted us permanent citizenship of the heavenly Jerusalem. We've done nothing to deserve it—we can't claim any of the credit. Our pride rebels against that. But true joy is found only when we point to our King in humble gratitude.

❷ How will you model this humble, joyful gratitude today?

JONAH: Runaway prophet

When God gives a message to his chosen servant, surely they will listen and obey? Not Jonah.

The book of Jonah is a joy for those who teach the Bible to children. With its giant fish and dramatic action, generations of children have been gripped by its story. But the danger is when we grow up, we leave the story behind. The reality is that Jonah is a book for adults too. Jonah teaches us big truths about the God of the Bible for our good and transformation.

Jonah is a God story

The book of Jonah primarily is a book about God—Jonah is mentioned 18 times, but God is referred to 38 times. So we're going to learn a lot about God and his character.

> ❷ *Look up Jonah 1:9, 2:9 and 4:2. What truths do we learn about God in these verses?*

Jonah is a real story

This is no myth. Jonah is a real prophet from the history of Israel. His preaching ministry was during the 8th century BC in the time of King Jeroboam II (see 2 Kings 14:23-25). Jesus also said that in some strange way he was like Jonah (see Matthew 12:40-41). More on Jesus and Jonah later.

Jonah is a grace story

Grace is the big theme in this book. Jonah received grace himself, but as we'll see, he just couldn't cope with the hated Ninevites

receiving the same grace God had shown to him.

Read Jonah 1:1-3

> ❷ *What did God command Jonah to do and why?*
> ❷ *What does this teach us about God?*
> ❷ *How did Jonah respond?*
> ❷ *What was Jonah trying to do?*

At the time, Nineveh was the capital of the feared Assyrian kingdom, the arch-enemy of God's people. The Assyrians had a reputation for ferocity and ruthlessness. They would later sweep the whole of the northern kingdom of Israel away into exile (see 2 Kings 17:5-6). Jonah was commanded by God to preach to the enemy. So he ran as far as he could in the opposite direction. Nineveh was a few hundred miles east. Jonah tried to go a few thousand miles west to Tarshish (in Spain)!

☑ Apply

We might think Jonah is foolish for running from God. But when have *you* heard God's word and deliberately tried to ignore it?

> ❷ *Why did you try to ignore God, and what was the result?*

Spend some time praying that God would speak to you through Jonah, and that you would have the humility to listen and obey.

Down into the depths

Is it really possible to run away from God? Jonah tried, but failed spectacularly.

....

The teeth of the storm
Read Jonah 1:4-10

❷ *Jonah looks like he's in control, but who does the writer say is really in control (v 4)?*

Read Jonah 1:17, 4:6, 4:7 and 4:8

❷ *What do each of these verses tell us about God's sovereign control throughout the story of Jonah?*
❷ *How do the sailors respond to the storm (v 5-7)?*
❷ *What does Jonah say to the sailors when they question him?*
❷ *Why is his answer ironic given what he's trying to do?*

Jonah tries to flee, but all he does is go deeper into trouble, literally! He goes *down* to Joppa, *down* into the boat (v 3), *down* into the hold (v 5) and then *down* into the sea; and eventually he goes *down* the gullet of the great fish. It shows the utter folly of trying to run away from the God who made the heavens and the earth. God is no small "godlet". He's the Lord of the universe!

🔽 Apply

Jonah discovers that we can't outrun God.

❷ *How might this be an encouragement to you if you are facing seemingly overwhelming difficulties and fears?*

❷ *How might this be a challenge to you if you are running away from God or not obeying him in some area of your life?*

Man overboard!
Read Jonah 1:11-17

❷ *What do Jonah's words in verse 12 show about his understanding of the situation?*
❷ *Follow through the story of the sailors. How do they react in v 5, 10, 14 and 16.*
❷ *What progress do they make in their understanding of God?*
❷ *Look up Jonah 2:8-9 and 3:6-9. How are the sailors similar to Jonah and the people of Nineveh?*
❷ *What does this teach us about God's love and mercy for all people?*
❷ *What does it show about God's sovereignty in using even a disobedient prophet for his purposes?*

🔼 Pray

Thank God that he is the Lord of the Heavens and Earth and that there is nowhere we can go and no situation we can face where he is not there with us.

Pray honestly about an area of your life where you might be running away from God. Ask God for grace to trust him and obey.

Grace experienced

Before preaching God's grace to others, Jonah first has to experience it for himself.

We left Jonah at the end of chapter 1 in the depths of the ocean. He'd run from God and was now facing certain death. But God provides a huge fish to swallow him up and keep him in the depths of its belly for three days and three nights. The poetic prayer in chapter 2 is Jonah's reflection on the events of those days. As we think about his submarine meditations, we'll understand how Jonah's experience points to a much greater rescue we can all experience.

The "death" of Jonah

Read Jonah 2:1-7

❓ *How do the images Jonah uses to describe his experience help to explain his situation and feelings?*

❓ *Jonah says he was banished from God's sight (v 4). How does this phrase reveal Jonah's biggest problem?*

❓ *What does Jonah say he did in verses 2 and 7 which led to his rescue?*

⌄ Apply

❓ *Jonah has to admit his need before he can be rescued. Why is this so important, and how is it true for us too?*

❓ *Why do we often find it hard to admit our need of God's help?*

❓ *In what ways have you seen this attitude in friends or family who aren't Christians?*

❓ *Why is this attitude dangerous both for unbelievers and believers?*

The rescue of God

Wonderfully, Jonah experienced God's grace when he cried for help.

Read Jonah 2:8-10

❓ *What lessons does Jonah give us in these verses?*

❓ *What does Jonah determine to do from this time on?*

···· **TIME OUT** ························

Read Matthew 12:38-41

❓ *In what ways does Jesus liken himself to Jonah?*

❓ *What is he challenging his generation to do with his preaching?*

❓ *In what ways is Jesus "greater than Jonah"? Why is ignoring his message so dangerous?*

⌃ Pray

Sometimes it's easy to forget just how amazing our rescue by Jesus is. When we forget the depths of sin we were in, we become complacent about what we've received in Jesus. Spend some time now thanking God for his rescue in Jesus. Think of two close friends or family members who haven't experienced this rescue—and pray they would come to know Jesus' grace too.

Bible in a year: 1 Samuel 17-18 • 2 Peter 2

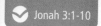

Grace proclaimed

Jonah gets a second chance to do what God commanded. This time the results are spectacular!

Jonah sank to the depths, but God raised him up in a miraculous way. Jonah knew that God was the "God of heaven, who made the sea and the dry land" (1:9). Jonah has experienced God sovereignly providing a giant fish to save him from the sea (1:17) and then commanding that fish to vomit him up onto dry land (2:10). Jonah has now experienced the grace of God himself. And he said in Jonah 2:9 that he would make good his vow and say, "Salvation comes from the LORD". In chapter 3, he gets a second chance to do this.

Jonah obeys

Read Jonah 3:1-4

- ❷ *How do verses 1-3 compare with what we read in Jonah 1:1-3?*
- ❷ *How does the description of the city in 3:3 highlight Jonah's task? Remember that Nineveh was the capital of Assyria: Israel's arch-enemy.*
- ❷ *What was Jonah's message?*
- ❷ *Why did God give Jonah this message? Look back to 1:2.*

⌄ Apply

Before we see the response of the Ninevites, think about God's dealings with Jonah.

- ❷ *In what ways is God's word to Jonah in 3:1 a remarkable act of grace to the prophet?*

- ❷ *How do God's dealings with Jonah offer us encouragement when we slip up?*

God's grace in Nineveh

Read Jonah 3:5-10

- ❷ *What are the results of Jonah's preaching in verses 5-6?*
- ❷ *What does the king ask his subjects to do in verses 7-9?*
- ❷ *How does God respond in verse 10?*

⌄ Apply

God uses Jonah's preaching to remarkable effect in Nineveh. We shouldn't be surprised since we have already witnessed the pagan sailors turn to God for mercy (1:16). Salvation truly comes from the Lord (2:9).

- ❷ *So why are we surprised, and perhaps unsettled, when God grants repentance and mercy to truly wicked people?*
- ❷ *Are there people today that you think are beyond the mercy and grace of God?*
- ❷ *If you're honest and the answer is yes, why do you think that? What does this tell you about your heart?*

⌃ Pray

We'll think more about this when we get to chapter 4. For now pray that your experience of God's grace would lead you to share that grace with others, without prejudice.

Jonah's problem

How would you feel after a successful outreach event where many people became Christians—delighted no doubt?

Jonah's mission to Nineveh had been a great success. His preaching was used by God to bring about the rescue of many. God "did not bring on them the destruction he had threatened" (3:10). But...

The grumpy prophet

Read Jonah 4:1-4

❷ *What is Jonah's reaction to the news about the Ninevites repenting (v 1)?*

❷ *Notice what Jonah did at the start of verse 2. Why is this a good thing for him to do, even in the mood he's in?*

❷ *What does it teach us about the sorts of things and feelings we can bring to God?*

❷ *In verse 2, Jonah gives his reason for being annoyed. What is it?*

❷ *What did Jonah expect God to do when he preached in Nineveh?*

❷ *Why was Jonah confident that God would do this?*

Jonah's big problem

From the start of our studies in Jonah we have seen that God's character is the key point. He's the Judge (1:2), the Creator (1:9), the Saviour (2:9), and the gracious and compassionate God, slow to anger and abounding in love (4:2). Jonah knew all this—and yet he ran off in the opposite direction. The key question is why?

To help understand this we're going to look at the prophet Nahum who wrote 150 years after Jonah and foretold the fall of Nineveh in 612 BC. These verses give an insight into what the people of Nineveh were like.

Read Nahum 3:1-5

❷ *What does God say the city is like?*

❷ *What is God's response to the people of Nineveh?*

❷ *How might this help to understand how Jonah reacted when told to preach God's message to the people?*

⌄ Apply

In Jonah's time, the Ninevites were just as ruthless as in Nahum's time. But through Jonah, God amazingly offered repentance—even to an ungodly people like the Ninevites. That's what Jonah couldn't stomach. In fact, he'd rather die than see them be saved (Jonah 4:3).

❷ *Why did God offer Nineveh rescue? (Remember Jonah 4:2!)*

❷ *Why do you think Jonah was happy for himself to be rescued but not the Ninevites? Is he right?*

❷ *What sort of people might you think are beyond God's rescue, or don't deserve it?*

❷ *Why do you think that? Is it right to think that?*

❷ *How might you be more like Jonah than you first realised?*

God's lesson

When you've received God's amazing grace, why wouldn't you want others to receive it too?

That's the big lesson at the end of Jonah—in fact that's what the whole book is about.

Remember what we've discovered so far.

- **Chapter 1:** Jonah runs away from God, ignoring his word. Through his disobedience pagan sailors worship God!
- **Chapter 2:** Jonah is rescued by God, though he doesn't deserve it.
- **Chapter 3:** Jonah preaches in Nineveh, and the Ninevites repent and receive God's mercy, though they don't deserve it.
- **Chapter 4:** Jonah learns the lesson that God's grace is free for all as God sovereignly wills. Who are we to keep it to ourselves or think we deserve it more than others?

Training the prophet
Read Jonah 4:5-9

- ❓ *What is Jonah still expecting to happen in verse 5?*
- ❓ *How does God show Jonah grace in verse 6?*
- ❓ *What is Jonah's reaction?*
- ❓ *What does God do in verses 7-8?*
- ❓ *How does Jonah react now?*
- ❓ *Compare verses 3-4 with verses 8-9. Why does Jonah want to die in both cases?*
- ❓ *What does his anger reveal about his heart?*

A strange ending?

We saw Jonah's issue with grace yesterday. He can't stomach God's grace to the Ninevites, but wants grace for himself and gets angry when God takes the shade from him. But the book ends with a question.

Read Jonah 4:10-11

- ❓ *What is God's point in verse 10?*
- ❓ *How does he force home his point (v 11)?*
- ❓ *Why do you think the book ends here?*

☑ Apply

The book of Jonah ends on a cliff hanger! We don't know what Jonah did next—but we can decide how *we* will respond. The danger is that our pride could get in the way!

- ❓ *How has Jonah challenged your attitude to others and their need of grace?*
- ❓ *In what ways are you more like Jonah than you first realised?*
- ❓ *What have you learned or been reminded of about God in Jonah?*
- ❓ *If you could sum up the message of Jonah in one sentence, what would you write down?*

⌃ Pray

Pray about your answers to the questions above. Pray that God would soften your heart so that you can offer grace to all people, not just to those you think deserve it.

The grass is not greener

Are you ever tempted to think that life would be better for you if you weren't a Christian?

The riddle
Read Psalm 49:1-6

- ❓ *For whom is this psalm relevant (v 1-2)?*
- ❓ *Why is it worth listening to (v 3-4)?*
- ❓ *What problem is the writer dealing with (v 5-6)?*

The writer is in trouble, facing injustice from those who are richer and more successful than he is. It's a universal problem—whether we're facing a corrupt government, belligerent colleagues or snide comments from friends, it all hurts. But the writer of this psalm isn't despondent. On the contrary, he's fearless, because God has equipped him with true wisdom—the ability to see his situation in the light of eternity.

The solution
Read Psalm 49:7-14

- ❓ *What reasons does the psalmist give for why we don't need to fear gloating oppressors? • v 7-9 • v 10-12*
- ❓ *What will happen to these people when they die (v 13-14)? Why?*

No matter how rich or successful someone is, there's absolutely nothing they can do to prevent death! Plastic surgery, health fads, world-renowned doctors—none of it ultimately makes a difference. Those who have trusted in themselves will discover too late that they are woefully ill-equipped to meet their Maker.

True success
Read Psalm 49:15-20

- ❓ *What will happen to the writer when he dies (v 15)? Why?*
- ❓ *How should v 16-20 affect the oppressed? How should they affect rich oppressors?*

What a contrast! Eternal life with God (v 15), or eternal separation from God (v 19). In light of these two destinies, the significance of worldly "success" just vanishes.

Re-read Psalm 49:7-9,15

- ❓ *How does Jesus fulfil these verses?*

It's impossible for one person to ransom another, because we're all bankrupted by our own sin. We can't "afford" it. And so Jesus' perfect life was the only payment great enough to free us from the grave. God had to do it for us. And he did.

☑ Apply

- ❓ *In what situations do you struggle with envying non-Christians? How does this psalm help you in this?*
- ❓ *How will knowing that Jesus has redeemed you eternally encourage you when you feel like a failure?*

☒ Pray

Talk to God about your answers to the apply questions, and ask him to give you the psalmist's biblical perspective on life.

Bible in a year: 1 Samuel 27-29 • 1 Timothy 3

2 KINGS: A fresh start?

We met both good and bad rulers in 1 Kings—but learned to trust in God's good and faithful word. 2 Kings starts with Ahaziah son of Ahab as the king of Israel. Is this an opportunity for a fresh start?

Read 2 Kings 1:1-18

1 Kings 22:51-53 briefly describes Ahaziah's reign: he reigned for two years and was evil like his father. In 2 Kings 1:1 we read that Moab has rebelled, a sign that the kingdom David and Solomon built is falling apart.

❷ *Where does Ahaziah put his trust in verses 2 and 3?*

❷ *How does God respond to Ahaziah's behaviour in verses 3 and 4?*

Notice how Elijah is able to turn the messengers round with his word from God (v 5), and how they faithfully report his message to the king (v 6). However, the king does not repent, rather he seeks to find out the identity of the man: it is Elijah (v 7-8).

❷ *What do you think Ahaziah is trying to do in verses 9 and 11?*

Twice Ahaziah sends troops after Elijah with a command, and twice those troops are destroyed by the hand of God (v 10-12). Just as happened earlier with the prophets of Baal in 1 Kings 18, God acts in judgment on those who oppose him, and his prophet.

❷ *Why doesn't fire from heaven come down a third time in 2 Kings 1:13-15?*

❷ *Why is the prophecy repeated a third time in verses 16 and 17?*

Ahaziah has no son, so he is succeeded by his brother Joram. Notice that we are told very little about Ahaziah, other than how he died (v 18).

☑ Apply

2 Kings 1 is hardly a fresh start. Ahaziah is just like his father, putting his trust in Baal-Zebub (which literally means "Lord of the Flies", probably a deliberately mocking variation on Baal-Zebul, "Baal the Prince"). Despite all of Elijah's efforts, and despite all that God has done, Israel's kings still trust in Baal, rather than in God. There might be a few faithful Israelites around like the third captain of 50, but things look bleak. However, God is still sovereign. He is the one who is in charge of life and sickness and death, not Baal-Zebub.

☑ Pray

Give thanks to God that he is still sovereign in all situations, even when we live in a time and a culture where God is widely ignored.

Pray for patience and wisdom to trust in God's lordship, even when times are hard.

Passing the mantle

Elijah passes the prophetic mantle to Elisha, who demonstrates his credentials as an anointed successor to Elijah's powerful ministry.

....

Swing low
Read 2 Kings 2:1-18

Elijah knows he is about to be taken up to heaven (v 1), and so do the prophets, and Elisha (v 3, 5).

> ❷ *Why do you think Elisha tells the prophets to be quiet in verses 3 and 5?*

Elijah goes from Gilgal, to Bethel, to Jericho and then to Jordan. Three times Elisha refuses to stay behind (v 2, 4, 6). Then Elijah parts the waters and crosses the Jordan, to reach his final destination.

> ❷ *What do these verses reveal about Elijah the prophet?*
> ❷ *What do we discover about Elisha's character here?*

Elisha asks for a double portion of Elijah's spirit in verse 9. A double portion is what the first-born son would receive; Elisha is simply asking to inherit Elijah's ministry, not to be twice as powerful as him.

> ❷ *How do we know that Elisha's request is acceptable to God (v 10, 11)?*

Elisha mourns Elijah's passing in verse 12 before the prophet is taken up to heaven in a whirlwind. Elisha knows his mentor is not coming back.

> ❷ *Look back at verse 8. Why does Elisha do what he does in verses 13 and 14?*

The company of the prophets recognise Elisha as Elijah's successor (v 15). However, they still want to search for Elijah, and aren't yet quite ready to trust the word of the new prophet in town, leading to a fruitless search for Elijah's body (v 16-18).

Sweet water
Read 2 Kings 2:19-25

Elisha is in Jericho, and there is a problem with the water.

> ❷ *Why do you think Elisha threw salt, as well as proclaiming God's word in verses 20 to 21?*

We have seen the curse on Jericho before, in 1 Kings 16:34. It dates back to the conquest and Joshua 6:26. Here the curse is reversed.

Elisha demonstrates his authority as God's prophet but not everyone is convinced. Elisha heads to Bethel, the place where Jeroboam had set up one of his golden calves in 1 Kings 12:25-33.

> ❷ *Who are the boys mocking when they jeer at Elisha, and why is the judgment on them so harsh (Deuteronomy 18:19)?*

⌄ Apply

The prophetic word here offers hope, but also judgment, and calls for obedience. Our challenge is to be ready to receive God's word, whether it is a promise of joy, or a call to costly obedience and sacrifice.

Moab is revolting

Elisha now begins his ministry to Israel's kings in earnest. He has his work cut out for him…

Thirsty work
Read 2 Kings 3:1-27

❷ *What kind of king is Joram in v 1-3?*
❷ *Why do you think Joram is so keen to act against Mesha (v 4-6)?*

Jehoshaphat comes along for the fight, as does the king of Edom (v 7, 9). They head through the desert but run out of water.

❷ *What do you make of Joram and Jehoshaphat's attitude to the LORD and his prophet in verses 10-13?*

Elisha only speaks because Jehoshaphat is there (v 14). He brings his message in an unusual way, through the playing of a harpist (v 15). The means are unusual, but the message is clear.

❷ *What does the prophecy tell us about how God provides for his people (v 16-18)?*

Israel will bring destruction on Moab (v 19). The prophecy comes true in the next verse.

❷ *How does the promise of water and the promise of victory come together in verses 21-24?*

···· **TIME OUT** ····························

Verses 24-25 emphasise the destruction Israel brings on Moab. **But look at Deuteronomy 20:10-20.**

❷ *Is this how Israel was supposed to wage war?*

Fearful fightback

King Mesha tries to rally the troops, but initially fails (v 26) Then in his desperation, he offers his son as a sacrifice, forcing Israel to withdraw.

❷ *What explanations might you give for what happens in verses 26-27?*

We are told that "the fury against Israel was great" in verse 27, but we are not sure *whose* fury. It might be the fury of the Moabites inspired by their leader, or God because of the way that the Israelites have conducted this war. We are not sure.

▾ Apply

There are times when the precise details of what is happening in the Bible are unclear. However, we can see from the context that God is in charge of what happens here, and that the prophetic word that Elisha spoke proves to be true. God's word is clear, even if every little detail isn't.

❷ *How should we respond when we don't understand every detail of a Bible passage?*
❷ *How does Elisha's ministry here encourage us when we come to difficult passages?*

God's good gifts

Like Elijah, Elisha brings not only wisdom or judgment to Israel's leaders but also blessing to God's faithful people.

Providing for the needy
Read 2 Kings 4:1-7

We read about two miracles today. First, the widow's oil.

> ❷ *Why might the woman mentioned in verse 1 expect Elisha's help?*

The woman is in a desperate situation, and only has a small jar of olive oil left.

> ❷ *What does this miracle require of the woman?*
> ❷ *Why do you think the door of the house was shut in verses 4-5?*
> ❷ *How does God's provision here honour this woman (v 6)?*

Just as Elijah provided food for the widow of Zarephath (1 Kings 17:8-16), so Elisha provides for the widow of one of the prophets.

> ❷ *Elisha's miracle takes place in the land and involves the company of the prophets. What does that suggest about how Elisha's ministry differs from Elijah's?*

▲ Pray

Give thanks to God for the way he provides for his people in their need.

Providing for the provider
Read 2 Kings 4:8-17

In many ways, this woman is the opposite of the poor widow we met in verses 1-7.

> ❷ *How does the Shunammite demonstrate her commitment to God in verses 8-10?*

Elisha wants to help the woman in some way, so he offers to do something for her when he is staying in the chamber she has provided. (We also meet Gehazi for the first time in verse 12; we'll meet him again in chapter 5.)

> ❷ *What do we learn about the woman's character in 4:13-14?*
> ❷ *Why do you think the woman is hesitant to believe Elisha in verse 16?*
> ❷ *Read Genesis 18:9-14. How are the two narratives similar?*

▼ Apply

God makes a promise to the woman through Elisha, and God keeps his promise to bless his people (2 Kings 4:17). We will see what happens next tomorrow, but here we are reminded of God's goodness to his people, even when the nation is going astray, and that there are still faithful people in Israel. God provides by his grace not just to those in obvious need, but to all those who trust in him.

▲ Pray

Reflect on your own life, and give thanks to God for the way in which he has provided for you.

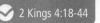

Life and death

Elisha has already given proof of his divine calling and status by the miracles he has done. He now demonstrates God's power over life and death.

A God of surprises
Read 2 Kings 4:18-37

A number of surprising things happen in these verses. The first is in verses 18-20: the child who was a very direct gift of God, dies.

- ❓ *Why do you think the woman acts in the way that she does in verses 20-25?*
- ❓ *What is surprising about Elisha's response to the situation in verses 25-27?*
- ❓ *What do verses 28 and 30 tell us about the woman who needs nothing?*

Gehazi is sent ahead by Elijah, but is unable to raise the dead, despite having Elisha's staff. We are not told why. Nor are we told why Elisha stretched himself out on the boy, (v 34-35) although Elijah does something similar in 1 Kings 17:17-24. Both accounts make it clear that the prophet prayed (2 Kings 4:33)—trusting in God's power to raise the dead. The boy awakes with a sneeze and is returned to his mother.

- ❓ *There are many strange things in this account. What puzzles you most about what God does here?*

☑ Apply

God has blessed the Shunammite woman, then seemingly takes that blessing away. Elisha doesn't have access to God's plans. Life can be confusing, but we are encouraged to trust in God's ultimate purposes.

The bread of life
Read 2 Kings 4:38-44

Two miracles demonstrate God's provision of food for his people.

- ❓ *Why do you think the gourds were added to the stew (v 38-39)?*
- ❓ *Why do you think Elisha adds flour to the pot (v 41)?*

A man bakes bread—the first of the harvest (v 42). Rather than taking it to the priests at the idolatrous shrine in Bethel, he brings it to Elisha, as the representative of the true Israel. It will be food for the people, but will it be enough (v 43)?

- ❓ *What does this miracle show about Elisha's relationship with God (v 43-44)?*

☑ Apply

Throughout 2 Kings 4, God has provided through Elisha for various people in various ways. Some of the miracles here may seem more significant than others, but they all show God's provision.

- ❓ *What do you think you need most at the moment?*
- ❓ *How does this passage help you to trust in God's provision for your life in the future?*

True and false Israel

Not all of Israel is truly Israel (see Romans 9:6). This passage shows what it means to trust and worship God—and the surprise about who is true and who is false.

Read 2 Kings 5:1-27

Naaman is a great man, but a leper; not modern leprosy, but some kind of undefined skin disease. In God's providence, an Israelite captive points to the possibility of a cure from the prophet (v 2-3).

❓ *Why is Naaman sent to the king of Israel with a present in verses 4-6?*

The king of Israel thinks it is a trap (v 7), but Elisha offers a cure—to wash in the River Jordan.

❓ *What does Naaman's response in verses 11-12 tell you about him?*

Another servant offers wisdom to his master; Naaman receives the treatment, and is healed.

❓ *What does this healing and the refusal of the gift demonstrate about God (v 15-16)?*

❓ *What does Naaman's request in verses 17 and 18 show about his character now?*

We may find Naaman's request in verses 17-18 strange, but Elisha is content with it; Naaman still had to serve his king, just as faithful men like Obadiah had to serve Ahab (see 1 Kings 18:1-16). Naaman is a faithful worshipper of God now.

❓ *What do Gehazi's actions reveal about his character in 2 Kings 5:20-24?*

Naaman may well have thought Elisha's initial refusal was politeness, and so is happy to be given a chance to contribute. However, this transaction undermines the gracious act of the prophet in healing Naaman and suggests God's favour could be bought. So Gehazi is punished.

❓ *What do Elisha's words to Gehazi in verses 25-27 teach you about God's knowledge, and his justice?*

⌄ Apply

This chapter is one of reversals. The great Naaman is only saved by the advice of two lowly servants and has to humble himself to wash in the Jordan. Yet in his humility he receives healing and salvation. Gehazi is privileged to be Elisha's servant but rejects those benefits for the sake of some money and some clothes. He receives his just reward.

❓ *What do you need to learn from the examples of Naaman and Gehazi?*

⌃ Pray

Pray for a heart of humble thanksgiving for God's grace, and to not take God's good gifts for granted.

Shrinking God

God made us in his image. But here his people stand accused of shrinking God—trying to control him by remaking him in their image.

Summoned
Read Psalm 50:1-6

- ❓ Who is being summoned?
- ❓ Who is being judged?
- ❓ How is God described here? What does this teach us about his right to judge?

Sacrifice or bribe?
Read Psalm 50:7-15

- ❓ Who is God speaking to (v 7-8)?

These are God's people, who seem to be following the sacrificial system to the letter. But their motives are all wrong...

- ❓ How have they misunderstood the purpose of the sacrifices (v 9-13)?
- ❓ What does this reveal about their relationship with God?
- ❓ What kind of sacrifice is God looking for (v 14-15)?

It's almost comedic—the idea that God is dependent on sacrifices, waiting for them hungrily! But the underlying point is much more serious: these Israelites think that God can be manipulated. They give him what he wants, and he'll give them what they want. They've missed the point entirely. Sacrifices weren't a bargaining chip to ensure an easy life—they were about restoring the relationship between God and his people. God himself is their reward.

☑ Apply

- ❓ Are there ways in which you try to manipulate God, doing deals with and making offers to him?
- ❓ Are there areas of life in which you desire God's gifts more than God himself?

The morality factor
Read Psalm 50:16-23

- ❓ Who is God speaking to (v 16)?

In other words, hypocrites, whose actions betray the truth their words try to hide.

- ❓ What evidence does God bring against them (v 17-20, 2)?
- ❓ What had they misunderstood (v 21)?
- ❓ What will the outcome be for them?

These Israelites have assumed that God is just as morally laid-back as they are. They've mistaken his silence for approval, and then forgotten all about him, presuming that he'll turn a blind eye.

☑ Apply

- ❓ Are there ways in which you shrink God to fit with your own comfortable ideas?

⌃ Pray

Spend some time repenting of your small view of God. Praise him for who he really is.

The power of the prophet

Elisha is involved in the big affairs of state—advising and intervening in wars and international affairs. But that doesn't mean he is unconcerned about the more ordinary details of daily life…

A minor miracle?
Read 2 Kings 6:1-7

- ❓ What encouragements might be drawn from the situation described in v 1-2?
- ❓ How is the working of God's providence demonstrated in verses 3-4?
- ❓ Why do you think Elijah makes the axe head float (v 5-7)?

☑ Apply

Compared to some of the other things Elisha does, this may seem a very minor miracle. Yet he meets a very real need. We are reminded of God's care through the prophet for the needs of his people, big or small.

Major misdirection
Read 2 Kings 6:8-23

The king of Aram, Ben-Hadad, is at war with Israel again.

- ❓ Why do you think Elisha warns Israel's king about the king of Aram's movements in verses 8-10?

The king of Aram suspects treachery, but his officers know it is Elisha (v 12). As so often in 2 Kings, the enemies of Israel have a better grasp of the power of the prophetic word than many in Israel. The king of Aram sends troops to surround Dothan.

- ❓ What does Elisha's servant need to see in verses 15-17?

TIME OUT
Read Matthew 26:53

- ❓ How does this compare with what Elisha and his servant see here?

God strikes the enemy with blindness (2 Kings 6:18) and Elisha leads them into the middle of Samaria, where they are surrounded by the Israelites, before opening their eyes.

- ❓ There is a lot in these verses about seeing. What did the king of Aram need to see?
- ❓ Why do you think the Aramean troops are spared and even treated with generosity(v 21-23)?

☑ Apply

The Arameans are released, and the raids stop, at least for a time. God has again delivered Israel through the words and actions of his prophet. He continues to care for the needs of his people, big and small. Also, we have been given a glimpse "behind the curtain" as we saw the chariots of fire in verse 17.

- ❓ How does this passage encourage you to recognise God's power, provision and care for you day by day?

The worst of times

Samaria faces a terrible siege and famine, but God promises deliverance.

....

War and famine

Read 2 Kings 6:24 – 7:2

Again Ben-Hadad attacks Israel, this time besieging the capital city, Samaria. Times are desperate, and the famine is great, so things which are almost inedible are sold for a great price (6:25).

> ❷ *What do you make of the king's response to the woman in verses 26-27?*
> ❷ *What does the woman's tale in verses 28-29 tell us about the physical, spiritual and moral state of Israel at this time?*

Back in 1 Kings 3 we met two women, and heard their dispute over a living and a dead baby. There, Solomon was able in his wisdom to bring justice. All this king has to offer is despair (2 Kings 6:30).

> ❷ *Why do you think the king blames Elisha (v 31)?*
> ❷ *What does verse 32 reveal about Elisha's standing before God and in Israel?*

The messenger comes down just as Elisha predicted. However, the king blames God, and gives up on God (v 33). God is clearly speaking through Elisha, but the king does not wish to listen anymore.

> ❷ *From what we have seen so far in 2 Kings, how should the king have been responding to the famine?*

Elisha promises that the price of food will fall the following day. However, the officer with the king cannot believe that such a thing could happen in verse 2, leading to a prophecy that will be fulfilled at the end of chapter 7.

> ❷ *Why do you think the sceptical response of the officer is such a problem here?*

⌄ Apply

It is the worst of times in Samaria, where the extent of the famine is tragically emphasised by the actions of the two women—actions which are also mourned in Lamentations 2:20 and 4:10 when Jerusalem is destroyed later. The king is helpless and hopeless. His officer shares his lack of faith. And yet Elisha still speaks the word of God, still promises deliverance, and has the ear of at least some of the elders of Israel.

> ❷ *What does this passage teach us about the reality of life in our world?*
> ❷ *How could this passage encourage you to find hope even in the darkest situation?*

Promises kept

God intervenes in the terrible war, and both of Elisha's startling predictions come true. Even in the most desperate of situations, God's promises are the only sure-fire certainty.

Read 2 Kings 7:3-20

The scene shifts to outside Samaria, and we meet some lepers.

> ❷ *What does the decision of the lepers tell us about the state of things in Samaria at this time (v 3-4)?*

The lepers find an empty camp (v 5). The Arameans have fled on the basis of a noise, which the Lord has caused. In 2 Kings 5 God cleansed a foreign leper. Here Israelite lepers come to the rescue.

> ❷ *Why do you think the lepers decide to tell others about what they have found (7:8-9)?*

⌄ Apply

The lepers are unexpected agents of deliverance, and in some ways slightly reluctant ones, at least at first. They are unclean and unnamed. And yet God uses these unlikely individuals to bring his plans to pass.

> ❷ *What good news could you share with the spiritually starving you meet today?*

Famine relief

The news that the Arameans have fled reaches the palace.

> ❷ *What does the king's response and the response of the officer in verses 12-13 tell us about their response to God's word?*

The king sends chariots in but not with any great hope. However, they discover that the Arameans have fled over the Jordan, and that there is plenty of plunder to be had.

> ❷ *What is emphasised in verses 16-17?*
> ❷ *Why do you think that the actions of the officer, and what happened to him, are retold in verses 18-20?*

⌄ Apply

The king and his officer find it hard to believe, but two promises are made by Elisha in 2 Kings 7:1-2, and both come true in these verses. One brings relief to Samaria, the other judgment on unbelief. The narrator emphasises that things happen according to God's word, and that the prophetic word should be trusted, and acted upon.

> ❷ *How does this passage encourage you, and challenge you to trust in God's word?*

⌃ Pray

Trusting in God's word can be challenging, especially when, humanly speaking, the situations seem so hopeless. And yet time and again, we have the evidence of God's promises kept to reassure us.

Reflect on the evidence you have seen for God's faithfulness in your life, and pray for confidence to trust in God's word.

Blessing and judgment

Elisha's reputation has spread far and wide. Even though he is God's prophet to his people Israel, it does not stop him from travelling further afield…

Reputation restored
Read 2 Kings 8:1-6

Some time has passed for the Shunammite woman and her family, who have been out of Israel during the famine—preserved by God's gracious word. She comes back for her land which has probably passed to the crown in her absence.

> ❷ *What surprises you about the scene we read about in verses 3-5?*
> ❷ *What means does God use to restore the Shunammite's land?*

⌃ Pray

Elisha is still the agent of blessing for the Shunammite woman, even when he is not present. In the midst of narratives about politics, kings and international conflicts, we are reminded that God is not just involved in the high affairs of state, but is also actively caring for the poor and needy.

Give thanks that we come in confidence to a God who provides, in detailed and specific ways for those he loves.

A painful promise
Read 2 Kings 8:7-15

> ❷ *What do verses 7 and 8 tell us about Elisha's reputation outside Israel?*

Hazael comes to Elisha with a gift and a question and receives a complicated answer (v 10). To understand it, we need to trace through the rest of the passage.

> ❷ *What does Elisha's weeping reveal about his heart in verses 11 and 12?*

Elisha tells Hazael that he will be king of Aram (v 13). This appointment has been a long time coming, as it was promised back in 1 Kings 19:15.

> ❷ *Why is Hazael anointed king, even though he will cause such sorrow in Israel?*
> ❷ *How does Hazael respond to the prophetic word in 2 Kings 8:14-15?*

Ben-Hadad's illness was not fatal, and he certainly could have recovered as Elisha said. He does die—but by the hand of Hazael, who probably made it look like an accident; either way Hazael becomes king.

⌄ Apply

In 2 Kings 8:1-15 God's providential hand is at work, but the means he uses are the "coincidences" of a meeting in the king's court, and a prophetic word that takes some time to work out. And yet God achieves his purposes.

> ❷ *How does God's sovereignty over Ben-Hadad and Hazael encourage you to have confidence in God as you think about international affairs in the world today?*

Bad blood in Judah

Meanwhile, back in the land, we meet the next two incumbents of the throne of Judah: Jehoram and Ahaziah.

Read 2 Kings 8:16-29

The scene shifts back to Judah after a long time away. We are following the pattern we have seen before—alternating between north and south, as the reigns of kings overlap. Jehoram, son of Jehoshaphat becomes king, and reigns for eight years. Jehoshaphat has been a good king according to 1 Kings 22:41-50. But what will his son be like?

❷ *What makes Jehoram a bad king, and why is Judah treated differently to Israel (2 Kings 8:18-19)?*
❷ *Why do Edom and Libnah (towns in Judah) rebel (v 20-22)?*

Jehoram scores a victory of sorts in Edom, (v 21), but it seems it only allows him to flee safely back to Judah (v 22). Whatever else he did (v 23), the key events of his reign relate to whether or not he was faithful to God. We then come to his son, Ahaziah (v 25).

❷ *What does the length of Ahaziah's reign (v 26) suggest about what kind of king he was?*
❷ *What problem does the writer highlight with Ahaziah's kingship (v 26-27)?*

⋯ **TIME OUT** ⋯⋯⋯⋯⋯⋯⋯⋯⋯⋯⋯

Read 1 Kings 11:1-8

❷ *How is the situation in Jehoram's reign and Ahaziah's reign similar, and how is it different from Solomon's time?*

Not only does Ahaziah follow in the idolatrous ways of the northern kingdom, he also joins in their battles, and so is in Jezreel by the end of the chapter—in the far north of Israel. This sets the scene for what comes in the next momentous twist in the story.

▾ Apply

This passage highlights two recurring features from the history of Judah and Israel. First, we see the continuing problem of idolatry, which so often in Judah is linked to relationships with Israel. Here, those relationships take the form of the continuing impact of the marriage alliance between the families of Ahab and Jehoshaphat. Second, we see the continuing grace of God to Judah. Despite the unfaithfulness of Jehoram and Ahaziah, God remains faithful to his promise to David, that one of his descendants would remain on the throne.

❷ *This passage indicates that close relationships can lead to sin.*
  • *How might you need to heed that warning?*
  • *How might you warn another Christian about this danger?*
❷ *How does God's continued faithfulness to an often faithless Judah encourage you to trust in God's mercy?*

Jehu the executioner

Jehu is anointed king and brings the long-awaited judgment on Ahab's family. But the story starts with the curious tale of a hit and run prophet...

The anointed king...
Read 2 Kings 9:1-13

Like Hazael in 2 Kings 8, Jehu is not of the royal line, but he will be king, just as was promised in 1 Kings 19:16.

> ❷ *Why do you think Elisha planned this as an "anoint and run" job?*
> ❷ *What do these verses tell us about why Jehu was made king?*
> ❷ *What does the response of the officers in verses 7-11 suggest about what kind of man Jehu was?*

These words may be new to Jehu, but we have been told about what will come to Ahab's house, for example in 1 Kings 19:15-18, and 1 Kings 21:21-24, after Naboth is murdered. God's word may not be fulfilled immediately, but it will be fulfilled.

... brings judgment
Read 2 Kings 9:14-37

> ❷ *How does God arrange things in verses 14-16 to make it easier for Jehu to rebel?*

Jehu rides for Jezreel, but Joram doesn't know why he is coming. Has there been a battle? Two horsemen are sent out, but neither return. Finally, the king himself heads out to find out what is happening.

> ❷ *How do verses 22-26 reinforce the fact that Jehu is God's agent of judgment?*

> ❷ *Ahaziah dies, shot through the heart by Jehu's arrow (v 27-29). Given what we know of him from 2 Kings 8, does that strike you as a just judgment?*

Jehu heads to Jezreel, where Jezebel meets him defiantly, comparing him to King Zimri who only reigned for seven days (1 Kings 16:15).

> ❷ *Why do you think we are told in detail about Jezebel's grizzly end?*

⌄ Apply

Judgment inevitably and inescapably comes on those who oppose God. It may seem hard to trust this when so many evil and wicked people perpetrate such terrible crimes on a daily basis. But God can be trusted to keep his promise to bring justice, as he does to Naboth here.

⌃ Pray

Give thanks to God that he is just, and that all evil deeds will one day be perfectly punished. It is not wrong to ask the Lord to hasten the day when this will happen.

Washing away my sin

"God, please forgive me, because…" How do you complete that sentence when you have sinned? It is one of the most important questions there is.

How we answer it reveals whether we have truly understood the gospel.

Helpfully, we know exactly what inspired David to write this psalm. 2 Samuel 11 – 12 lays bare the tabloid scandal. David committed adultery with Bathsheba and then had Uriah, her husband, murdered to cover his tracks. But God saw, and God sent his prophet Nathan to confront David. This is an intimate glimpse into the soul of a man who has been forgiven the most terrible sins.

No excuses
Read Psalm 51:1-6

❷ *What two aspects of God's character does David depend on in verse 1?*
❷ *How might these things make it easier for David to be honest before God about his sinfulness?*

I am the king of excuses. My first instinct is always to claim that things are not really my fault.

❷ *How does David show in verses 4-6 that he "owns" his sin?*

Cleanse me and change me
Read Psalm 51:7-12

❷ *What are all the things that David asks God to do in these verses?*

❷ *Have there been times when you have felt defiled and filthy because of your sin?*

How good to read of a God who washes us clean!

Hyssop (v 7) was used in cleansing ceremonies (Exodus 12:22; Leviticus 14:4-6, 49-52). It appears in the New Testament at a very significant moment that relates to the cleansing of sin: **read John 19:29.**

Serve with joy
Read Psalm 51:13-19

❷ *In verses 13-15, what does David do as a result of being forgiven?*

This is why one way to become a better evangelist is to spend more time thinking about my sinfulness: the more aware I am of how wonderful God's salvation and forgiveness are, the more keen I will be to tell others about what Jesus has done.

🔼 Pray

Psalm 51 teaches us to pray, "God forgive me because you are a God of unfailing love, whose Son has paid for my sin". What wonderful news for guilty sinners!

We should keep short accounts with God—it is healthy to confess our sins daily. Pray this as a psalm of confession before God, putting the verses into your own language and repenting of your particular sins.

Jehu's vengeance

Jehu's reign starts with bloody violence to eradicate the toxic line of Ahab. But what kind of king will he prove to be in the longer term?

The end of Ahab's line

Read 2 Kings 10:1-27

Jehu's work is not finished, as Ahab still has 70 sons. He writes to those who are looking after them, and discovers they will not act to protect them.

> ❷ *How do Jehu's actions and words in verses 6-10 serve to protect his throne?*
> ❷ *What motive does he give for this ruthless ferocity (v 9-10)?*

Jehu acts as God's agent of judgment, even if we might begin to suspect that his motives are not always pure.

> ❷ *Jehu kills Ahaziah's relatives in verses 12-14. Do you think he should have?*

Jehu makes an alliance with Jehonadab, son of Rekab (v 15-16), who seems to be the leader of popular opposition to Ahab's family. Thus, the word is fulfilled (v 17). He then turns his attention to the Baal worshippers, who he deceives into assembling.

> ❷ *Why do you think Jehu takes all the precautions he does in verses 20-24?*

The worshippers are cut down, the sacred stone destroyed, and the temple is turned into a latrine. Ahab's dynasty, and the vile religion he promoted have been completely destroyed.

> ❷ *What questions does this brutal narrative raise for you?*

The start of Jehu's line

Read 2 Kings 10:28-36

> ❷ *What is both good and bad about what happens next?*

Jehu destroys Baal worship, but he continues the false worship that Jeroboam set up, (v 28-29). One layer of idolatry is removed, but another remains.

> ❷ *How does God show his grace to Jehu and his judgment on Israel (v 30-33)?*

Twice we are reminded that Jehu followed the sins of Jeroboam (v 29, 31), and Hazael begins his work of cutting off parts of Israel. However, Jehu has a comparatively long reign of 28 years, and a son to succeed him.

✔ Apply

Jehu was used mightily by God to achieve his purposes, but he was still responsible for his idolatry, and the suffering he brought to Israel. Likewise, we need to understand how deep the temptation to idolatry remains within us. We may have experienced major "triumphs" in our lives, as we have rejected some big-picture idolatries—rejecting another religion perhaps, or conquering the love of money. And yet how easily other things move in: a love of comfort, a desire to indulge ourselves in our old age, etc.

> ❷ *What idols lurk unchallenged in your heart?*

Hanging by a thread

Jehu's actions in the north spark a similarly bloody transfer of power in Judah by Ahaziah's mother. The promised line of David is threatened, but God is at work…

Read 2 Kings 11:1-21

We return to Judah again, picking up from where we left off in chapter 8, and with the continuing problem that Jehoshaphat's marriage alliance with Ahab has caused.

> ❓ How does God preserve David's line in 11:2-3 from the gruesome granny?

Jehoida the priest organises a rebellion against Athaliah's rule, by taking advantage of the changing of the guard to station more troops around the king to protect him.

> ❓ What do verses 5-9 show about the kind of support Jehoida has?
> ❓ Why do you think the spears and shields of David are used in verses 10 and 11?
> ❓ What does the symbolism of the crowning in verse 12 tell you about what the king of Israel should be like?

Athaliah finds out about the conspiracy from the noise, but by the time she investigates it is too late, because not only does Joash have the support of the priests and the military, the people of the land are also rejoicing in the new king.

> ❓ What is ironic about her cry of "Treason! Treason!" in verses 13 and 14.

A covenant is mentioned in verse 4, in which the conspirators commit to overthrow Athaliah. Two covenants are mentioned in verse 17.

> ❓ What is the purpose of the various covenants made here?
> ❓ What is the wider significance of the use of covenant language?
> ❓ What does the narrator emphasise about the situation once Joash becomes king, in verses 19-21?

⌄ Apply

The promises God has made to David look like they might fail, but the acts of Jehosheba and the providence of God ensure survival. Jehoida the priest leads the people in restoring the king to his throne. We see here the way minor characters with a commitment to the Lord can have a major impact, as God achieves his purposes through his faithful people.

> ❓ You may consider yourself to be a (very) minor character in your church, your family, the kingdom of God; but how does this example encourage you to think about your initiatives and actions?

⌃ Pray

Give thanks that God keeps his promises, even in turbulent times and through painful and difficult situations.

Pray that God would use you as part of his glorious plan to bring glory to the one true King—Jesus.

Restoring worship

Joash and Jehoida repair the temple, but like all building projects, it quickly runs into trouble. The temple is being restored, but will the people's faith in God be restored too?

Rebuilding

Read 2 Kings 12:1-21

❷ *What kind of evaluation of Joash does the opening summary (v 1-3) encourage us to make?*

Money is then collected for the repair of the temple (v 4-5). Clearly there is a desire to place the temple at the heart of worship in Judah, despite the continued tolerance of high places. However, for whatever reason (bad management or corruption?) the repairs are slow to get going, and so the priests hand over responsibility to the king.

❷ *Why do you think we are given all these details about how the collection was organised in verses 9-12?*

❷ *How was the money spent (v 13-16), and, again, why all the detail?*

After a slow start, progress is made on repairing the temple. The priests don't lose their support and the workers are honest. All seems to be well in Judah. However, there is a snag. Hazael king of Aram is still a threat, and he attacks Jerusalem. So, Joash pays tribute to get him to leave.

❷ *How does verse 18 affect how we think about Joash, and his work to restore the temple?*

A 360 evaluation

❷ *What is surprising about verses 20-21?*

···· **TIME OUT** ·················

Back in verse 2, we were told of the importance of Jehoida for Joash's faithfulness. **Read 2 Chronicles 24:17-27.**

❷ *How does this passage help you understand why Joash was assassinated?*

The temple and the priests have been in the background in 2 Kings, but they will be increasingly important for the second half of the book.

☑ Apply

This passage highlights the importance of right worship. The people were to worship at the temple, not at the high places they had made for themselves. It also highlights that at the centre of right worship is heart worship: Joash turned away from God, and ultimately trusted in tribute rather than the Lord to save him.

❷ *How might you be tempted to forget that we are to worship God wholeheartedly, in the way he commands?*

The last days of Elisha

Back in the northern kingdom, we see the continuing impact of Elisha, even after the great prophet has died.

Repentance and respite
Read 2 Kings 13:1-9

- ❓ *What kind of king was Jehoahaz (v 1-2)?*
- ❓ *What do the events of Jehoahaz's reign remind us about how we are to respond to God (v 3-5)?*

We are not sure who the deliverer mentioned in verse 5 was. Perhaps it was the king, perhaps it was Elisha. Either way, God continues to be gracious to a very imperfect people, who remain ungrateful and persist in their worship of other gods. Jehoahaz dies, and his son follows him.

In just a few verses we see both the possibility and tragedy of the northern kingdom. The king turns to God in desperation and is saved, yet returns to the sins of Jeroboam.

⌃ Pray

Pray for a heart that remembers God's kindness and goodness to you in Jesus Christ, and that is always turned to God in repentance and faith.

The promise of life
Read 2 Kings 13:10-25

Jehoash becomes king, but he is just like his fathers and does evil. However, God is still keeping his promise to Jehu that he will have four generations on the throne, and Jeroboam his son succeeds him. We focus on a key event in Jehoash's reign.

- ❓ *Why do you think Jehoash comes to Elisha (v 14)?*
- ❓ *Why do you think Elisha gets the king to shoot an arrow in verses 15-17?*

The king only strikes the ground with the arrows three times (v 18). Perhaps the king was supposed to keep striking the ground until Elisha told him to stop. But now the victory will not be so great. Elisha dies and the country is in continued peril.

- ❓ *What hope does the miracle of verse 21 offer to Israel?*

Despite the tributes and bribes he has been sent, Hazael keeps oppressing Israel (v 22).

- ❓ *What is the basis for Israel's hope in verses 23-25?*

⌄ Apply

Elisha dies, bringing to an end an era of hope and restoration. Yet there is still hope for Israel in repentance (v 1-9); in God's promises to Abraham, and Israel; and in the reality of life after death.

- ❓ *How does this passage encourage and challenge you to find the right hope in the right place?*

Grace and folly

Two kings—Amaziah and Jeroboam II—show God's continued grace to his people, and the continued folly of their leaders.

Un-civil war
Read 2 Kings 14:1-22

Amaziah becomes king, following his father. This is a time of stability in Judah, and Amaziah is another generally good king of Judah.

❷ *How do verses 5-7 demonstrate Amaziah's wisdom?*

❷ *What does Jehoash's reply to Amaziah show about the relative strengths of the two nations (v 8-10)?*

Although Jehoash's reply to Amaziah is not very diplomatic, it does point to political realities and Amaziah's pride. It is no surprise that Amaziah is defeated.

❷ *How do verses 12-14 emphasise the humiliation Judah suffered?*

In the middle of Amaziah's reign (v 15-18), we have another summary of Jehoash, and then the rest of Amaziah's reign is dated in relation to Jehoash which suggests Judah was effectively a vassal of Israel. There is another conspiracy in verses 19-20, but Azariah his son still succeeds his father as king.

❷ *How do these verses demonstrate God's grace to Judah?*

Evil triumph
Read 2 Kings 14:23-29

Our attention now shifts north again to

Jeroboam II. He is another king like those before him (v 23-24), and yet during Jeroboam II's reign, God restored Israel's borders

❷ *Why did God rescue Israel during Jeroboams II's reign (v 25-27)?*

There are other achievements to mention in Jeroboam II's reign, including more victories. And God is still keeping his promise to Jehu as Zechariah becomes king.

⌄ Apply

Amaziah has a few good features, particularly at the beginning of his reign, but his pride leads to folly and humiliation. Jeroboam II is just like his predecessor Jeroboam, doing evil. And yet during this period, God shows his grace and mercy to Israel and Judah. It is a time of stability, when the borders of the kingdom extend. But neither in the face of God's judgment, nor in the face of God's mercy do his people turn back to him. We are prompted to ask: *how long will the Lord continue to bless his wayward people?*

⌃ Pray

Give thanks that God shows mercy to his people, even when they are far from him.

Pray that you would reject the folly of turning away from God, and find true wisdom in following Christ

Seven kings

Decline continues, as problems persist in north and south. A succession of kings—good, bad, ugly and compromised—demonstrate the downward trend to ruin…

Northern decline
Read 1 Kings 15:1-38

The pace of the narrative accelerates, as we move through around 60 years of kings in north and south.

> ❷ *How would you assess Azariah's reign (v 1-4)?*

We find out why the king was afflicted with leprosy in 2 Chronicles 26:16-20; in his pride the king tried to burn incense in the temple. We also learn of his co-regency with his son Jotham in 2 Kings 15:5. Although Azariah ruled for 52 years, he probably ruled with his father for some of that time, and then later with Jotham. This seems to have happened with other kings of Judah as well. Azariah dies and Jotham reigns, who we'll come back to at the end of the chapter.

> ❷ *What does the narrator emphasise in Zechariah's reign in verses 8-12?*
> ❷ *How does the reign of Shallum emphasise God's judgment on the sins of his people, and his faithfulness to Jehu (v 13-16)?*

Menahem brings some stability, despite his violence and sin (v 16-18). But now the king of Assyria comes onto the scene, and Menahem has to pay tribute to him, which works for the time being (v 19-20), but Assyria will become a big problem for Israel and Judah. At least Menahem manages to be succeeded by his son.

> ❷ *What does Pekahiah's reign in verses 23-26 indicate about the political and spiritual state of Israel at this time?*
> ❷ *How does Pekah's reign (v 27-31) show the pattern repeated, but also a downward spiral?*

Hedging your bets

During Pekah's reign, we return to Jotham son of Uzziah (=Azariah).

> ❷ *How does Jotham's reign repeat the pattern from Azariah, but with a downward direction (v 32-38)?*

▼ Apply

In Judah we meet two kings (Azariah and Jotham) who are not wholeheartedly devoted to God, the high places still remain. Perhaps they thought it was the path of least resistance to allow these false practices to continue. Perhaps they were hedging their bets. But things are much worse in Israel. The mighty Assyrian empire is on the horizon and seems unstoppable as conspiracy follows conspiracy. Worse than that, the sins of Jeroboam, the false worship which he set up in 1 Kings 12:25-33, continues to ensnare the king and the people. These are familiar sins, but they remain deadly ones.

> ❷ *How does this passage challenge you to take seriously your "familiar" sins, and to repent of them?*

Lies and deceit

We're entering a run of psalms that are unfamiliar to many of us, written in a situation that is profoundly alien to most of us—being pursued by enemies who want you dead.

But these songs will mature us spiritually as they take us beyond our own experiences. They will also help us to pray for the many Christians around the world for whom violent danger is a very real experience.

The context
Read 1 Samuel 22:1-23

A man named Doeg has betrayed David to King Saul (who wants him dead) and slaughtered the priests who helped David.

Lying lips
Read Psalm 52:1-4

Words have consequences. The first casualty in war, they say, is the truth. This is certainly the case in the Russia/Ukraine conflict— where systematic bare-faced lying has deceived an entire nation. These lies have caused untold misery for millions.

> ❷ *What terms are used to describe the words of David's enemy, and the impact those words have?*
> ❷ *Where have you witnessed the destructive power of words?*

Destined for destruction
Read Psalm 52:5-7

The wicked man grows proud as he does what he likes and it works. He flourishes like a weed in the garden, until God steps in, uproots him and tosses him on the fire.

> ❷ *What impact does this have on those who trust in God?*

Secure in God's name
Read Psalm 52:8-9

> ❷ *David has no kingdom, army or wealth; but how does he view himself in verse 8?*
> ❷ *Why does he feel so secure? Where does he place his trust?*

Jesus knows what it feels like to be betrayed, insulted, lied about and falsely accused. At his trial wicked words won the day and he was declared guilty and tortured to death on the cross. But three days later he rose to everlasting life. He shows us that although in the short term the wicked may flourish and the righteous may suffer, in the long term those who trust in God will flourish in his house for evermore.

✔ Apply

> ❷ *How do you respond when people lie about you?*
> ❷ *When do you find yourself wishing you could swap trust in an unseen God for something more tangible?*

Why not write out verses 8-9 and stick them where you will be reminded of their truths regularly?

Ahaz the innovator

National leaders who break the mould and are innovative are often remembered as successful. But Ahaz leads Judah into further decline with his worship innovations.

....

Read 2 Kings 16:1-20

The narrative slows down as we come to King Ahaz. However, this is not good news.

❷ *What makes Ahaz such a bad king (v 1-4)?*

Notice that Ahaz follows the example of the kings of Israel, but also goes beyond their evil practices with child sacrifice in verse 3. His foreign-policy decisions seem clever to start with but are ultimately disastrous.

❷ *Why might his choices here seem clever?*
❷ *What has he sacrificed, and why will that lead to ruin?*
❷ *Why does Ahaz decide to build an altar like the one in Damascus (v 10-11)?*

Ahaz starts to operate like the kings of the surrounding nations, as a kind of priest-king making offerings (v 12-13), and starting to move the "furniture" around in the temple to suit his preferences (v 14).

The new altar, designed in Damascus, is for burnt offerings, the old altar for guidance, and only for the king's use.

❷ *How does Uriah the priest compare to other priests we have met in 2 Kings?*

Ahaz makes other changes to the temple in 2 Kings 16:17-18. These are not just cosmetic, as the symbolism of the temple furnishings was given by God in 1 Kings 6 and 7 to testify to who God is, and who Israel should be.

❷ *Why does Ahaz make the changes he makes?*
❷ *How does 2 Kings 16:19-20 offer some hope for the future?*

⌄ Apply

Ahaz is certainly an innovator. He brings in lots of new practices and behaves like a priest-king. Why does he do this? Some of the changes Ahaz makes might result from pressure from Assyria, and some might be done to please Ahaz's saviour, the king of Assyria, but some of the changes seem to be made because Ahaz wanted to do it like this.

We do not worship at a temple with altars and offerings, but we do have a God who has told us how to worship him: in Spirit and truth, trusting in Jesus Christ and seeking to live as his obedient people.

❷ *How should Ahaz's behaviour act as a warning to anyone who wishes to change how we worship God?*

The last king of Israel

Despite all the politicking of Ahaz to keep the Assyrians sweet, there is an inevitability to what comes next. The end comes swiftly, as Assyria conquers and destroys Israel.

Ruin

Read 2 Kings 17:1-6

❷ *Given what is about to happen, what is ironic about the description of Hoshea in verses 1-2?*

❷ *Why is Hoshea described as a traitor (v 3-4)?*

❷ *Foreign nations have invaded Israel before. What is different this time?*

These verses explain the context for Israel's destruction: rebellion against Assyria and deportation. Israel had become a vassal state of Assyria, and while Hoshea wasn't the worst of Israel's kings, judgment has finally, inevitably come.

Reasons

Read 2 Kings 17:7-23

❷ *How is this passage a summary of what 2 Kings is trying to teach us overall?*

❷ *What details in verses 7-12 highlight the persistent, determined sin of Israel?*

❷ *How does Israel demonstrate that she is "stiff-necked" in her response to God (v 13-15)?*

Israel persistently refuses to turn back to God. It started with the calves that Jeroboam made back in 1 Kings 12, and then moved to Baal worship under Ahab. More than that, there is worship of the "starry hosts" and the child sacrifice mentioned in relation to Ahaz in 2 Kings 12. They have continued

to rebel for over 200 years despite constant warnings, and demonstrations of God's love for them.

❷ *What message should Judah take from these events (2 Kings 17:18-20)?*

❷ *Why did Israel go into exile (v 21-23)?*

❷ *How do these verses emphasise God's grace to and patience with his people?*

⌄ Apply

This passage emphasises the just judgment of God on his rebellious people. The agent may be the Assyrian king, but the cause of Israel's destruction is God's judgment on their continued sin. However, this passage also emphasises God's continued patience with Israel. How he brought them out of Egypt, placed them in the land, exhorted them to obedience, established Jeroboam as king, and continued to warn them through the prophets.

❷ *Are there aspects of your life that show the same stubborn ingratitude?*

⌃ Pray

Give thanks to God that he is a God who judges justly and fairly, and yet who shows great patience and mercy. In particular, give thanks to God for his mercy shown to us in Christ, who rescued us from judgment, and pray for a heart to hear and follow him wholeheartedly.

 Bible in a year: 1 Chronicles 13-15 • Luke 1:57-80

A new start in Samaria

With the Israelites deported, what will happen in the ruined northern kingdom of Israel? And are there any grounds for hope?

....

Read 2 Kings 17:24-41

One of the ways in which ancient empires controlled different people groups was by moving them around—detaching them from their homelands to neutralise the risk of an uprising, and to break their identity as a nation. So the Assyrian king brings in people from various other places to repopulate the towns of Samaria (v 24).

❓ *How do the new inhabitants of the land respond to God's correction (v 25-28)?*

This might look like a positive start but notice that the Lord is described as "the god of the land"; just one of many gods. Also, a priest from Bethel might not be the best person for leading people to worship God rightly, as Bethel was the home for one of the golden calves of Jeroboam. The people brought their own gods with them (v 29-31) and continued the kinds of practices that happened in the land before.

❓ *How do the new inhabitants of Samaria think about their gods (v 32-33)?*

The people are described as worshipping God, but at the same time (v 34) they are *not* worshipping the Lord.

❓ *What does verse 34 emphasise about what it means to worship the Lord?*
❓ *What is essential about God-honouring worship (v 35-39)?*

TIME OUT ....

This is the genesis of the despised Samaritans we read about in the New Testament. The issue of how to worship the Lord correctly remained an issue into Jesus' day, and is at the core of his conversation with the woman at the well in John chapter 4.

☑ Apply

These verses underline the tragedy both of Israel's failure to trust God as their rescuer, which ultimately led to exile, and of the new people of the land doing the same thing. The problem here is syncretism: worshipping God, and at the same time, giving honour and glory to other gods as well.

In the ancient world, people worshipped many different gods. In our world that is less common, but people will still seek to worship God, and trust in other things, in modern idols, for salvation as well: money, sex, power, family, leisure, education and the self, to name a few common ones.

❓ *How do you need to take seriously the call to worship God alone? Which of the modern idols mentioned above might be a problem for you?*

⌃ Pray

Pray for a heart that is devoted to God, and to worshipping him alone.

Hezekiah's faith

Israel was destroyed—so we might expect Judah to fall like the next domino. But it does not, because of the faith of one of Judah's greatest kings, Hezekiah.

Hezekiah's courage
Read 2 Kings 18:1-16

- ❷ *What makes Hezekiah such a great king (v 1-4)?*
- ❷ *What is the result of Hezekiah's obedience (v 5-8)?*
- ❷ *Why are we reminded of what has just happened to Israel (v 9-12)?*

Finally! A king who removes the high places, and other idols. No wonder he is able to rebel against Assyria and win many victories over the Philistines. Here is a king who listens to what Moses commanded, who will trust in God, not in foreign rulers.

- ❷ *How does Hezekiah respond to the Assyrian threat (v 13-16)?*

☑ Apply

Faced with an Assyrian army, Hezekiah pays tribute. It is costly, and involves stripping the temple, which is never a good sign. He has faith in God to act against idolatry, but he still fears the king of Assyria. Like Abraham, or David, and like us, he has moments of weakness, and his faith is not perfect.

- ❷ *How can we draw encouragement from the example of Hezekiah?*

Confidence trick
Read 2 Kings 18:17-37

Despite the heavy tribute, Sennacherib still comes up against Jerusalem. He may well have intended to remove Hezekiah as king, just as Hoshea and other rebellious kings were removed by Assyria before.

- ❷ *The Assyrian king sends his officers (v 17). What does that suggest about how he treats Hezekiah?*
- ❷ *How does the king of Assyria rightly challenge Hezekiah about what he is relying on (v 19-25)?*

After a brief interchange with Hezekiah's officials the commander addresses the people directly.

- ❷ *What does the king of Assyria claim to be able to offer the people (v 28-32)?*
- ❷ *Why doesn't the king of Assyria expect the Lord to deliver Judah (v 33-35)?*

The people are silent, and the officials return to Hezekiah (v 36-37).

☑ Apply

The king of Assyria asks the right question: *Who should you trust in?* He is right that it is not Egypt, and not horses. However, because of the Assyrian king's "success" he doesn't trust in God, but in himself. We will see the consequences of this in 2 Kings 19.

- ❷ *What challenges do you face to your faith from the "successful" things you have achieved?*

Hezekiah's deliverance

It's a tense moment. A massive army is arrayed against Jerusalem—the odds seem impossible. Except when you have God on your side...

Seeking the Lord
Read 2 Kings 19:1-19

❓ *How does Hezekiah respond to the threat (v 1-4, 14-19)?*

God promises deliverance through the prophet Isaiah, because of Assyria's words against the Lord (v 5-7). In verse 8 there is a temporary reprieve, as the field commander leaves Jerusalem, but the messengers come again in verse 9.

❓ *Why is it argued that Hezekiah should abandon his trust in God (v 10-13)?*
❓ *What is Hezekiah's confidence based on?*
❓ *Why should God deliver him?*

▼ Apply

As in 2 Kings 18, Hezekiah *begins* well by seeking out Isaiah the prophet. But he also *continues* well, in praying to God in the temple. He is an example here of persistent faith. He also shows us how to pray with confidence, because of who he knows God *is*, and by seeking God's glory in his prayers.

Sennacherib's fall
Read 2 Kings 19:20-37

❓ *Why will Zion and Jerusalem mock Assyria (v 21-23)?*
❓ *Why has the king of Assyria achieved his victories (v 23-26)?*

God will judge the king of Assyria for his insolence. The punishment will fit the crime; the Assyrians often led captives away with hooks and bits in their mouths, but now the same will happen to them (v 27-28).

❓ *What does the sign described in v 29-31 promise to Hezekiah and the people?*
❓ *Why won't the king of Assyria bring a siege against Jerusalem (v 32-34)?*
❓ *How is Isaiah's prophecy fulfilled (v 35-37)?*

The events of verses 36 and 37 are about 20 years apart, but they show how God keeps his promises.

▼ Apply

God acts in judgment on the Assyrians in verse 35, in one of the most astonishing acts of God in the whole Bible. God acts to rescue Hezekiah, he acts for the sake of his promise to David, but most of all God acts for the sake of his own name and reputation. God judges the king of Assyria who challenged and mocked God's authority. We can be confident that God will act for the sake of his name.

⌃ Pray

Pray now for the things that concern you—world affairs, your family, your church. But appeal to the Lord to act so that his glory will be revealed through the answers he gives.

Pride and poultices

Hezekiah's trust in God earned a reward for himself and his people, but it only delayed the coming judgment. There is a bleak future for Judah.

Power over death

Read 2 Kings 20:1-11

Hezekiah receives word that he is about to die in verse 1.

❓ *Why does Hezekiah pray as he does?*

God answers Hezekiah's prayer immediately, before Isaiah has left the building (v 4).

❓ *Why does God heal Hezekiah (v 5-6)?*

Notice that God promises deliverance from Assyria (v 6). It seems as if the events of chapter 20 take place before chapter 19. The mechanism for healing is mundane—a poultice made from figs. This perhaps explains why Hezekiah seeks another sign in 20:8.

❓ *How would the sign that Hezekiah receives in verses 9-11 reassure him that he would recover?*

⌄ Apply

Again Hezekiah demonstrates a living faith in God, and persistence in prayer. He is confident in God, and in his own righteousness. This isn't a claim to perfection, but to the general right behaviour that we have seen from Hezekiah in the last two chapters.

❓ *How does this encourage you to pray?*

A hopeless future?

Read 2 Kings 20:12-21

At the same time, envoys come from Babylon. Hezekiah shows them his storehouses in verse 13, probably because they are discussing an alliance against the king of Assyria. Isaiah then questions the king about their visit in verses 14-15, which becomes an occasion for a prophecy.

❓ *What does the future hold for the king of Judah (v 16-18)?*
❓ *What do you make of Hezekiah's response in verse 19?*
❓ *What does the final summary of Hezekiah's reign in verses 20-21 tell us about him as a king?*

⌄ Apply

Isaiah looks forward to a time when Babylon will threaten and overwhelm Judah. Hezekiah is a great king, but even though his life is extended, he still eventually dies. Judah needs more than a great king like Hezekiah or David, she needs a perfect king. In his life and death, Hezekiah points us to his greater descendant, Jesus.

⌃ Pray

Give thanks that we have a King who has done all that we need, and who can rescue us from all dangers even death.

Fools seldom differ

If we all agree, we must be right—right? But in the 1700s, most people agreed it was fine to trade people as slaves. In first-century Jerusalem, the majority agreed Jesus must die.

True wisdom is not found by looking out and listening to others, but looking up to God, and listening to his word, the Bible.

The context

We're not told what event in David's life prompted this psalm. But Psalm 52 fits 1 Samuel 22 and Psalm 54 fits 1 Samuel 26. In between, in 1 Samuel 25, is the account of David and Nabal, whose name means "fool", and who more than lived up to his name in what we read...

The madness of crowds

Read Psalm 53:1-3

"The fool" in the Bible is not a joker, but the person who lives their life in a way that ignores the fundamental realities of the world. The fool thinks having an affair won't harm their marriage, or that they'll get rich if they spend all their money on lottery tickets. The ultimate foolishness is to think we can live well and wisely while not recognising the reality of God. So the fool of verse 1 is just an extreme version of what all of us are like.

Devouring others but consumed by fear

Read Psalm 53:4-5

❷ *What sort of behaviour results from denial of God in verse 4?*

❷ *How secure are these powerful people who crush and devour others, according to verse 5?*

The hope of the world

Read Psalm 53:6

When we look around at a world where wicked fools seem to get ahead and cause suffering to so many, then, like David, we long for God to establish his rule. When we stop looking out at others and look at the selfishness and bitterness and pride and ugliness in our own hearts, then we long for him to send salvation. Unlike David, we can look back to the day when that salvation was achieved, through Jesus' death on the cross.

⌄ Apply

❷ *When, and in what way, are you tempted to be "a fool"—to ignore God's word and do things that he says are unwise and wrong?*

❷ *What things in the news or in your life at the moment make you long for the return of Jesus to bring justice and salvation?*

⌃ Pray

Pray that you would trust God, rather than be foolish. Be honest with him about specific ways in which you need his help to do this.

Bible in a year: 1 Chronicles 28-29 • Luke 4:31-44

Is this the end?

After Hezekiah's death, tragedy returns to Judah as she turns away from God under the ungodly leadership of Manasseh and Amon.

Detestable

Read 2 Kings 21:1-26

Manasseh becomes king, and has a long reign. But it seems that all the lessons learned under the inspirational leadership of Hezekiah have been forgotten.

> ❓ *How is Manasseh's reign worse than what has come before (v 2-6)?*

Manasseh is worse than Ahab, doing all the detestable things that previous kings of Israel and Judah have ever done, and then adding some more.

> ❓ *Why do you think the writer of 2 Kings highlights the Asherah pole in the temple (v 7-8)?*
> ❓ *What are the king and the people like now (v 9)?*

God speaks to his prophets about Manasseh (v 10).

> ❓ *What is the judgment that is going to come on Judah (v 11-14)?*
> ❓ *Who is to blame for this (v 11, 15)?*

We are told in verse 16 that Manasseh shed much innocent blood. We are not told whose, but this may well be a reference to the blood of prophets.

> ❓ *Manasseh has a long reign and dies in peace (v 17-18). Given what he did, does this seem fair?*

Like father, like son…

Manasseh's son Amon comes to the throne.

> ❓ *What was Amon like as king (v 19-22)?*
> ❓ *Does the death of Amon offer any hope?*

✔ Apply

After Hezekiah's reign, the era of Manasseh and Amon represents a swift, tragic, and it would seem irreversible decline: Judah would go into exile, because she has behaved just like Samaria, and just like the nations who were in the land of Canaan before Israel.

In these two reigns we see God's character displayed. He is patient with his people, giving them time to turn from their sins, even if that means Manasseh has a long reign when it looks like God isn't doing anything. He is gracious to his people, still speaking to them through the prophets, despite their rejection of his word. And yet he is also just and does promise judgment on those who continue to rebel against him.

> ❓ *As you live in the world today, how does God's character as revealed here offer you a challenge and also comfort?*

Reforming zeal

It is nearing the end for Judah, but one of her final kings brings renewal and hope—and it all starts with a "chance" discovery.

Lost and found

Amon's son Josiah has been mentioned twice already in 2 Kings 21. Now we come to his reign.

Read 2 Kings 22:1-20

❓ *How is Josiah assessed (v 1-2)?*

Josiah becomes king aged eight, so it is no great surprise that it is not until the 18th year of his reign, when he is aged about 26, that he begins to restore the temple. The money is distributed, and the work begins.

❓ *Why do you think the temple needs to be restored?*

Hilkiah finds the Book of the Law (v 8) and this book is read to the king by Shaphan the secretary. We are not certain about the identity of this book, but it may have been Deuteronomy.

❓ *Why does Josiah tear his robes (v 11-13)?*

Josiah is receptive to God's word. He listens, and he wants to know more. So, he consults the prophet Huldah; female prophets were rare in Israel's history, but not unknown.

❓ *What is going to happen to Judah and why (v 15-17)?*
❓ *What is the grace that God extends to Josiah, and why does he receive it (v 18-20)?*

Josiah models what it is to be a true king. He restores the temple as the place where people can come and worship God. He listens to the word of God and responds with repentance to the challenge of that word. God is gracious to him, and he will be buried in peace.

❓ *How does the example of Josiah challenge you as you encounter God's word each day in Scripture and at church and in Bible studies?*

⌄ Apply

Despite the reforms that Josiah brings, and we will read more about them in 2 Kings 23, God's judgment will still come on Judah, and the people will still go into exile. While individual Israelites still turn to the Lord, it is too late for the nation. There is a warning here not to assume that there will always be some future time when people can turn back to God. The time for repentance is *always* now.

⌃ Pray

Pray for those you know who have not yet turned to God, that they will realise the need to turn to him in the present.

And if there is some unresolved, unrepented sin in your life—now would be a good moment to do something about it...

Josiah's reforms

Josiah leads the people back to God, reforming and restoring worship even in Judah's final days. They will go into exile with a renewed sense of who they should be.

Reforms in Jerusalem
Read 2 Kings 23:1-14

Josiah's reform efforts continue, beginning with the renewal of the covenant. The Book of the Covenant contains the promises of God, and the king and people commit themselves to the Lord.

❓ *What does this covenant-renewal ceremony tell us about what lies at the heart of Israel's worship now?*

Josiah then begins the process of removing idolatry and idolatrous practices.

❓ *How is the thoroughness of what Josiah does emphasized (v 4-7)?*

He then moves out from the capital into the countryside (v 8-12).

❓ *Why was it important to remove the high places?*
❓ *How do Josiah's actions in verses 10 to 12 demonstrate the problem of idolatry and false worship in Judah?*

⌄ Apply

The tragedy of Judah's long-term faithlessness is revealed in these verses, particularly in verses 13 and 14, where we find that places of false worship have been in use since the time of Solomon.

❓ *How do these reforms encourage you to recognise the justice of God's actions?*

The limits of reform
Read 2 Kings 23:15-30

Josiah's reforms take him beyond the borders of Judah, to Bethel in verse 15. Here we see the fulfilment of the predictions made about Bethel back in 1 Kings 13 come true.

❓ *What do these verses demonstrate about how the word of God works?*
❓ *Why do you think Josiah killed the priests as well as desecrating the shrines, (2 Kings 23:19-20)?*
❓ *What do the celebration of the Passover and Josiah's further reforms show about him as king (v 21-25)?*

⌄ Apply

Josiah is unquestionably a great king. Possibly the *greatest* king of Judah. And yet judgement will still come. Josiah dies fighting against Egypt (v 29-30) and as we shall see his reforms die with him. We saw with Hezekiah that we need a perfect king. Here with Josiah, we see that we need an eternal king, one who will reign for ever. For all his glories, Josiah points us to his greater son, Jesus.

⌃ Pray

Give thanks that we have an eternal King, Jesus.

Bible in a year: 2 Chronicles 7-9 • Luke 6:1-26

The beginning of the end

Judah is weak and at the mercy of foreign powers as she experiences the full force of God's judgment for her repeated acts of wilful disobedience…

Spiralling down
Read 2 Kings 23:31 – 24:7

❓ *Jehoahaz follows Josiah. What kind of king was he (23:31-32)?*

❓ *How do verses 33-35 emphasise the power of the pharoah in Judah at this time?*

Jehoiakim follows after Jehoahaz's brief reign. As a king he is no better (v 35-36). He faces a new threat in Babylon in 24:1, just as Hezekiah was told in 20:12-21. Jehoiakim becomes Nebuchadnezzar's vassal, but then rebels.

❓ *Why do raiders come to destroy Judah (24:2-4)?*

Jehoiakim lasts for 11 years and is followed by his son, Jehoiachin.

❓ *What does verse 7 mean for Judah?*

☑ Apply

We get a glimpse of the movements of powerful empires in the ancient near east —Babylon and Egypt, just as before we encountered Assyria. We can see why these empires wanted to control the strategic location that was Judah, at the same time we see that their actions are permitted by God, who is ultimately in control.

It can feel scary when the news is filled with stories of huge-scale geopolitical events. But we can be confident that God is sovereign over all the nations, to achieve his purposes.

Exile begins
Read 2 Kings 24:8-20

Jehoiachin is just like previous kings of Judah, by doing evil.

❓ *Previously, the king of Babylon has been happy to take tribute from Judah. Why do you think he now takes the king prisoner and the people into exile (v 11-14)?*

❓ *What do verses 15-16 emphasise about who has been taken into exile?*

Egypt has appointed a king of Judah, now Babylon does the same (v 17). Again, a name is changed to indicate who is really in charge. He is not much of a king, more of a puppet.

❓ *So why do you think Zedekiah rebels against the king of Babylon (v 20)?*

☑ Apply

The process of dismantling Judah begins. Key people are taken into exile, and the king is an appointment by the king of Babylon. Again, we are reminded why this is happening: God is angry with his people for their continued sin against him.

☑ Pray

As we see God's justified anger at sin, give thanks that in Christ we have one who has died in our place, and taken that anger on himself.

Bible in a year: 2 Chronicles 10-12 • Luke 6:27-49 ❤

Into captivity

Zedekiah's rebellion is the final straw, and Nebuchadnezzar lays siege to Jerusalem to punish his rebellious vassal.

Complete catastrophe
Read 2 Kings 25:1-21

- ❓ *How severe was the siege (v 1-3)?*
- ❓ *What do the final events reveal about Judah's leadership at this time (v 4-6)?*
- ❓ *How do these verses show the hopelessness of the situation for Judah and Jerusalem when faced with the might of the Babylonians?*

Zedekiah is punished for his rebellion. It is a cruel punishment, highlighting the fact that although the Babylonian king is the agent of God's judgment, he is not a godly man. We have seen this a number of times in 2 Kings, with Babylon, Assyria, and earlier with Syria. God can use those who are not just to bring about his justice.

- ❓ *What are the key moments in the destruction of Jerusalem (v 8-11)?*

Jerusalem is systematically destroyed, and the people of Jerusalem go into exile, with just a few peasants left to work the land. Judah as a nation is no more.

The action then slows down in verses 13 to 17, as the objects taken out of the temple are described. Everything goes, whether gold or silver or bronze.

···· **TIME OUT** ····································

Read 1 Kings 7:13-51, where the temple furnishings mentioned here are described in more detail.

- ❓ *How does this passage help underline the tragedy of what happens in 2 Kings 25?*
- ❓ *What does the removal of the bronze indicate about what happens to the temple, (v 13, 16-17)?*
- ❓ *Why do you think the people mentioned in verses 18-21 are executed?*

☑ Apply

And so Judah goes into captivity. It has been inevitable for some time, and here we see the totality of the destruction brought to Judah: the king, the city walls, the temple, the leaders and the people. Nebuchadnezzar has dealt with a rebellious vassal, and at the same time, God has judged a rebellious people. God has been astonishingly patient through centuries of indifference, abuse and downright disobedient evil. He has shown time and time again that he is quick to give mercy, and slow to judge, but his patience has finally run out.

- ❓ *How does the destruction of Jerusalem help you to understand God's promise to judge when Jesus returns?*
- ❓ *How does the destruction of Jerusalem help you to reflect on God's grace, patience and mercy?*

↗ Pray

Pray for opportunities to talk to friends and family about the mercy and justice of God.

What happened next?

The aftermath of destruction is messy. In the closing of 2 Kings, we get a glimpse of what happened next to those left behind, and perhaps detect a glimmer of hope.

The hopeless
Read 2 Kings 25:22-26

- ❓ *Why do you think Nebuchadnezzar appoints Gedaliah?*
- ❓ *What do these verses suggest about Gedaliah's character?*

Ishmael assassinates Gedaliah, presumably hoping that somehow his royal blood will enable him to gain from doing this.

- ❓ *How does verse 26 underline the folly of Ishmael's action?*

···· TIME OUT ····

You can read more about what happened here, and Gedaliah's character, in **Jeremiah 40 – 41**. (Warning: it's pretty gruesome.)

✔ Apply

This brief record of what happens after Judah goes into exile underlines the continuing folly of God's people. They ignore the prophets—we read in Jeremiah 42 that they should *not* go to Egypt—and they make bad political decisions. They are hopeless; they have no real hope in God, and they are not able to save themselves.

⌃ Pray

Talk to the Lord about your own big life decisions. Where are you placing your trust for these things?

The hope?
Read 2 Kings 25:27-30

These final verses of 2 Kings deal with events that happened about 25 years after the destruction of Jerusalem. Jehoiachin, who went into exile back in 2 Kings 24:12, is released from prison.

- ❓ *What does Jehoiachin receive that indicates the kindness of the new king of Babylon?*
- ❓ *How does this kindness underline the situation of Judah at this time?*

✔ Apply

Jehoiachin's release from prison isn't much. The people of Judah are still in exile, and he is still effectively a prisoner of the king of Babylon, even though he is well treated. He will die in Babylon. And yet at the same time, it does underline that God has not forgotten his promises to David, made all the way back in 2 Samuel 7:7-17, that David will have a descendant who will rule over Israel for ever. The line of David's descendants is frail, but the promise does not fail. Jesus is of course the ultimate hope of 2 Kings: that one day a true, perfect and everlasting King will rule.

⌃ Pray

Pray for a heart to trust in the hope of our eternal King, Jesus.

Bible in a year: 2 Chronicles 15-16 • Luke 7:31-50

When wronged, pray

What do you do when you are seriously wronged? How do you react when you suffer real injustice, like your spouse cheating on you or business partner stealing from you?

Many Christians have a Jekyll-and-Hyde response. In public, we wear a good Christian mask and talk about seeking to forgive. But inside, we are a seething cauldron of resentment and anger. In an interview on the Psalms with U2 lead singer Bono, Eugene Peterson said, "We have to find a way to cuss without cussing". In other words, in a world where there is genocide and child abuse and adultery, we need language to express our (rightful) anger and longing for justice that is brutal enough to convey the depths of what we are feeling, and yet is not sinful. The psalms of vengeance enable us to do that.

The context of Psalm 54 is that David and his men have rescued the Ziphite villages from attackers. And yet now the people who owe David their lives have betrayed him to King Saul. So once again David must flee— **read 1 Samuel 23:19-20; 26:1.**

Save me
Read Psalm 54:1-3

❷ *How serious is David's predicament?*
❷ *What does he ask God to do?*

Slay them
Read Psalm 54:4-5

We delight to read verse 4 and it would be good to pray that we would be as confident as David when we are facing real dangers.

Most of us find verse 5 less comfortable. But remember, this is not David saying he will take vengeance with his own hands; this is him praying to God to do it. There is all the difference in the world. It is so much easier to let go of our own desire to take revenge when we know that God can be trusted to bring perfect justice (Romans 12:19).

Sacrifices for you
Read Psalm 54:6-7

❷ *How will David respond to God when he is saved?*

David knows he will be delivered because he has God's promise that he will reign as king of Israel. We do not have specific promises from God about being delivered from sickness and struggles in this life, but we do have his promise that we will be delivered through death to eternal life with Jesus. David offers sacrifices to express his gratitude to God.

❷ *What might be appropriate "freewill offerings" from us when we experience God's answers to our prayers, do you think?*

Apply

❷ *How does this psalm need to impact the way you respond to being mistreated?*
❷ *How will it impact the way you pray for others who are suffering injustice?*

THE BIBLE PLOT

Don't you think it would help us to understand the story of the 66 books of the Bible if there was a single verse that explained the plot? There is! It's Genesis 3:15.

Footnotes?

Read Genesis 3:15

Alfred North Whitehead was famous in England as a mathematician, but more famous in the United States as a philosopher. He once cleverly wrote that the simplest summary of Western philosophy is that it is a series of footnotes to the writings of the Greek philosopher Plato. We can adapt Whitehead's words to Scripture: the simplest summary of the Bible is that it's a series of footnotes to Genesis 3:15.

The end of the beginning

Genesis 3:15 marks the end of Act 1 of the drama of the Bible's story. There are more acts to follow. But in Act 1 there are three scenes already: the creation of the cosmos (chapter 1); the creation and purpose of Adam and Eve in particular (chapter 2); and now the tragedy of their sin (chapter 3). We are so used to living in a fallen world—the world between Genesis 4 and Revelation 22—that it's natural to feel life has always been the way it is today. We need to be reminded that it wasn't always like this, nor was it meant to be like this.

···· TIME OUT ····························

Read Matthew 19:3-8

When asked a question about divorce Jesus made it clear that he always thought from first principles. And one of these was to ask the questions: *What was it like at the beginning? How did God intend things to be?* If we don't do that, we may look at life back to front. And we may even begin to think about God the wrong way round. We may draw the wrong conclusions about what he is like from the mess we've made rather than from the world he made in which he made sure that everything was "very good" (Genesis 1:31).

Read Genesis 1:26-31

❷ *What high privilege did God give us when he created us (v 26-27)?*
❷ *How much did God give Adam and Eve (v 29)?*
❷ *What word describes God's attitude to them (v 28)?*

☑ Apply

Think about everything you have in this world. The resources you have, the privileges you enjoy, the abilities you have.

❷ *In what ways does Satan seek to obscure God's generosity to you?*

⌃ Pray

Lord, help me to taste and see that you are good today.

Crafty devil

Genesis 3 doesn't say the serpent was the devil. But certainly Jesus, Paul, and John believed he was. And what he says and does here are certainly devilish.

Genesis 3 is one of the Bible's most detailed accounts of temptation. And there is a lot we can learn both about the nature of temptation and—by observing the failure of our first parents—how to guard against it. But we mustn't lose sight of the fact that Genesis 3 is a description of one momentously significant event in human history, what is usually referred to in dramatic terms as "The Fall". It is a sobering story.

A devilish scheme

Read Genesis 3:1-7

The New Testament identifies the activity of the serpent with the work of Satan (see John 8:44; Romans 16:20; and especially Revelation 12:9; 20:2). The serpent was "more crafty than any other beast" (ESV). "Crafty" is not in itself a bad word in the Bible; usually it's used in a good sense (three times in Proverbs 14, in verses 8, 15 and 18, ESV). It means knowing the best way to accomplish your goals. However mysterious the figure of Satan seems to be, he is clearly...

1. God's creature,
2. characterized by evil purposes in opposition to God,
3. incapable of overcoming the sovereign God but...
4. intent on marring his glory.

The object of his attack is therefore the loving Creator's creatures and (for obvious reasons) those he has made to bear his family likeness, the man and the woman who are his "image" and "likeness" and also "blessed" (Genesis 1:26-28).

Sin summarised

Paul gives us the most condensed and yet the most profound biblical summary of what happened in the Garden of Eden.

Read Romans 5:12-21

❓ *What does Paul mean when he says, "Sin entered the world through one man"?*

❓ *How did he know that death was the result of sin?*

❓ *How can he say that "death came to all people" because "all sinned"?*

☑ Apply

❓ *How should Paul's statement that through sin we have "fallen short of the glory of God" (Romans 3:23, ESV) fill us with compassion for non-Christians?*

☒ Pray

Lord, help me to sense the tragedy of the human condition—that we have sinned and fallen short not only of your law but of your glory which you created us to admire and enjoy.

The woman deceived?

Some people get upset with Paul for writing 1 Timothy 2:14: "And Adam was not the one deceived; it was the woman who was deceived". Are they right? Or are they wrong?

The Bible doesn't explicitly tell us why the serpent approached Eve first. But it's not hard to guess. What is the quickest way to a husband's heart? What would give the devil the greatest leverage to draw Adam away from trusting, loving and obeying his heavenly Father? The answer is surely the best gift God had given him, his "helper". Yes, the woman who had become "half" of who he was: *Eve.*

Satan is so devilish—he seeks to use God's best gifts in order to get the leverage he needs to destroy our relationship with God.

Eve outwitted

Back to Paul's words about Eve for a moment. *Deceived?* Who dares say so?

Read Genesis 3:13

Paul was simply quoting what Eve said about herself! Apparently, Adam sinned with his eyes open. But someone was pulling the wool over Eve's eyes.

Paul warns us against being outwitted by Satan and says that "we are not unaware of his schemes" (2 Corinthians 2:11). But are we? We certainly see some of them in this passage.

Read Genesis 2:16-17 and 3:1-3

We sometimes say, "The devil is in the detail" and we see that here if we pay careful attention.

❓ How did the "crafty" serpent distort what God had said in Genesis 2:16-17 (3:1)?
❓ Is it significant that Eve's response adds to what God had said in Genesis 2:16 (3:3)?
❓ Why do you think the serpent said what he did in Genesis 3:4?

☑ Apply

❓ In what ways do you think Satan uses similar strategies in our lives today?
❓ Can you think of a time when you have been pulled in with the same lies?

TIME OUT

Read James 1:14-16. Perhaps when James wrote these words, Genesis 3 was at the back of his mind. Certainly, his words are an instructive commentary on how the serpent deceived Eve.

❓ How did he entice her by desire (v 14)?
❓ How did desire conceive and give birth to sin (v 15)?
❓ How did sin give birth to death (v 15)?

⌃ Pray

Our Father in heaven, lead us not into temptation, but deliver us from the evil one. Help us to be on our guard against the devil who uses your best gifts to entrap us.

Why blame Adam?

Doesn't it seem strange that although Eve was the first to take the forbidden fruit, in the New Testament it's Adam who is blamed?

Silence wasn't golden

❷ *Where was Adam when Eve was eating the forbidden fruit?*

Have you ever noticed that Genesis 3:6 tells us explicitly—and significantly that she took of its fruit and ate, and she also gave some to her husband *who was with her.*

You mean Adam was there? Why did he not say something! Why did he not stop her? Was there ever such a dereliction of duty—the duty of friendship, the duty of a husband, even were he a total stranger he knew what God had said! Eve did wrong; but she was deceived (she said so herself). She was blinded by the god of this world (2 Corinthians 4:4). He sinned with his eyes open.

"In Adam's fall we all sinned"

So, Adam's sin was multi-layered: he sinned by not warning and protecting his wife; he sinned by joining her in eating although he was the one to whom God had spoken directly. He was the fountainhead of the whole human race (even Eve was "descended" from his rib cage!). And so, Paul says that it is "in Adam" all sinned, and "in Adam" all died.

He had personally received God's word (Genesis 2:16). It was as clear as crystal. He failed to guard Eve, his best friend and

God-given helper; he then chose the path of her deceit rather than the path of obedience to God. It has always been better to obey God rather than man; and in this case it was better to obey God rather than the woman who gave some to her husband who was with her.

⋯⋯ TIME OUT ⋯⋯⋯⋯⋯⋯⋯⋯⋯⋯⋯⋯⋯

Read 1 Corinthians 11:2-8

Try to focus in these verses not on Paul's specific applications but on his two foundational statements: "the head of the woman is man" (v 3); and "woman is the glory of man" (v 7).

❷ *If verse 3 is true, how did Adam fail—and how do husbands today similarly fail?*

❷ *If verse 7 is true, what else does that tell us about the seriousness of Adam's failure?*

⌄ Apply

❷ *Do you remain silent when you should speak? When?*

⌃ Pray

Lord, you have given us wonderful gifts; help us to protect them and to guard our own enjoyment of them.

 Bible in a year: 2 Chronicles 25-27 • Luke 9:37-62

The blessed curse

Genesis 3:15 is sometimes called the protoevangelium—the first announcement of the gospel. But have you noticed it comes in the form of a curse?

Actions have consequences

Read Genesis 3:8-13

The "blame game" began with Adam and Eve. He blamed her (v 12); she blamed the serpent (v 13). They hid from God (v 8) and avoided his questions (v 9, 11, 13). How foolish to think they could hide physically or spiritually from the all-seeing God!

Read Genesis 3:14-24

Eve would experience pain in childbirth (verse 16a); her relationship to Adam would become warped (verse 16b). He would encounter inbuilt resistance to his task of gardening the earth for God's glory. Made from the dust to govern it, he would now himself become dust (v 19).

Salvation surprise

God's word to the serpent (Genesis 3:15) is the oldest and most-difficult-to-keep promise of salvation in the Bible. It comes in a surprising way—in a four-stage curse on the serpent!

- **Stage 1:** Hostility between the serpent and the woman
- **Stage 2:** Enmity between his offspring and Eve's offspring
- **Stage 3:** Conflict between him ("your") and one specific seed of the woman ("his")
- **Stage 4:** Victory when the coming seed

crushes the serpent's head while his own heel is crushed.

Old Testament believers shared in Christ's salvation by trusting in the promised, but not-yet-come, Deliverer. We share in it knowing that he is "Jesus, for he will save his people from their sins" (Matthew 1:21).

Merciful God

God is compassionate to two sinners. He gives them clothes (Genesis 3:21); he prevents them from eating the tree of life and confirming themselves permanently in their fallen condition (v 22-24). But he did something even more remarkable. By cursing the serpent, he blessed them—and us.

Each time we see an outstanding figure in Genesis, we hope it will be the serpent-crushing seed of the woman, but each time we are disappointed. Cain, Noah and Abraham all failed significantly. Many centuries would pass before the promise was fulfilled (see Galatians 3:13).

Apply

❓ *Do you hide from God or divert his questions when he probes your conscience?*

Pray

Thank you, Lord, for keeping your promise!

The end of the story

We must never forget that we ourselves are caught up into the Bible's story of the ongoing conflict between the seed of the serpent and the seed of the woman.

The long conflict

Read Genesis 3:15

> ❷ *What do you understand by the promise that there will be "enmity" between the serpent and the woman's seed?*

The truth of this verse is unfolded in the rest of the Old Testament: there is conflict between Cain and Abel, Pharaoh and Moses, Jericho and Joshua, Goliath and David, Babylon and Jerusalem. It reaches its climax in the ministry of Jesus; and it will rumble on through history until "Babylon", the city of this world, is destroyed (Revelation 18:1-24) and the city of God, the new Jerusalem appears (Revelation 21:1 – 22:5). Christians always live in a conflict zone.

The denouement

The climax of this conflict is described in the Gospels, developed in Acts, explained in the Epistles, and dramatically portrayed in Revelation. It emerges in Herod's destruction of the infants; it continues when the Spirit leads Jesus into the wilderness to withstand Satan; it is seen in the vast numbers of demons who mustered forces to attack the Lord Jesus. They knew he had come to destroy the works of the devil (1 John 3:8)—and them (Matthew 8:29). The final act of this drama opens when Satan enters the heart of Judas Iscariot (John 13:2) initiating the hour of the power of darkness (Luke 22:53). But by his incarnation, his tasting death for us, and his making propitiation for our sins, Christ has delivered us from the devil and will bring us back to the glory we have forfeited (Hebrews 2:9-10, 14-15). As Martin Luther's great hymn says: "For us fights the Proper Man, Whom God himself hath bidden"! Adam and Eve were defeated. Now in Christ we are "more than conquerors through him who loved us" (Romans 8:37).

Some homework

As you read through Scripture, note down the nature of any "conflict narrative" or comment. Then, sometime, connect these references on a timeline from the Fall to the victory of Christ. Then read and reflect on John 12:31-33; Romans 16:20; Colossians 2:15; Ephesians 6:10-20; and 1 Peter 5:8-11.

❯ Apply

Paul says we are not to be outwitted by Satan "for we are not unaware of his schemes" (2 Corinthians 2:11).

> ❷ *How have you found that to be true in your own experience?*
> ❷ *How to guard against his schemes?*

❮ Pray

Lord, thank you so much for the victory of Jesus! Help us to resist the evil one and to know we are conquerors!

 Bible in a year: 2 Chronicles 30-31 • Luke 10:25-42

Neither fight nor flee

Can you recall a time when you were utterly overwhelmed by problems and could see no possible way out? What did you do?

If I had wings...
Read Psalm 55:1-8

❷ *What is happening?*

David was a mighty warrior who fearlessly faced down the giant Goliath. But...

❷ *What does he wish he could do (v 8)?*

The sum of all fears
Read Psalm 55:9-15

❷ *Where does David face danger?*
❷ *Who is his enemy here?*

9/11 was terrifying because the great skyscrapers that crumbled before our eyes were such emblems of our security. Likewise, the means of their destruction were not fighter jets but passenger planes, which we use to go on holiday, for business travel, or to see distant family. This shattering of security is what David is facing: the city was the place of safety and security in ancient times, and close friends are the people he (and we) should be able to trust above all else.

So when we read in verse 9 that there is "violence and strife in the city", and in verses 12-13 that it is David's "close friend" who has betrayed him, we realise that the rug really has been pulled from under his feet.

The God I can trust
Read Psalm 55:16-23

The verses move back and forth between God and David's enemies.

❷ *What does David know that God will do for him if he calls on him?*
❷ *This section is bracketed by verses 16 and 23. What is David's resolution?*

Both verses declare his commitment, his trust in God. It's easy to overlook the little phrase at the start of verse 16—"as for me". He has seen his closest godly friend turn away from God, but he refuses to give up on God. He will keep on trusting.

Jesus taught that the Psalms pointed to his own sufferings (Luke 24:26-27, 44). So this psalm gives insight into what it felt like for Jesus to be betrayed by his close friend: **read Matthew 26:20-25, 45-50.**

❷ *How does this help you think more deeply about Jesus' sufferings?*

⌃ Pray

Fight or flight? When people turn against you, how do you respond? David the warrior wished he could fly away. But the right response is neither lashing out nor running off; it is calling on and trusting in the Lord.

"Cast your cares on the LORD and he will sustain you; he will never let the righteous be shaken." (Psalm 55:22)

❷ *What cares do you need to unburden yourself of today?*

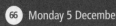

NUTSHELL GOSPEL

If I gave you the challenge to express the gospel in as few words as possible, how many do you think you could whittle it down to? 50? 20? 12? Ok—how about 7!

Mysterious gospel

That's what Paul does in the opening chapter of his letter to the church in Colossae, and we're going to spend the week digging into and understanding this single phrase.

Read Colossians 1:23b-27

> ❷ *What is Paul's mission in life?*
> ❷ *How does he describe his relationship to the gospel message?*
> ❷ *Why do you think he calls the gospel message a "mystery"?*
> ❷ *What seven-word phrase does he use to summarise the "mystery" of the gospel?*

Paul is picking up some of the language of the mystery cults that were common in the Roman world at this time. Adherents were initiated into "secret knowledge" that was supposed to give them "fullness", lift them to a higher spiritual plane, and open up eternal life for them. There were, for example, cults to the Egyptian gods Isis and Osiris, and the mystery cult of Mithras was popular among Roman soldiers. Freemasonry is a modern example of this type of cult.

Paul is saying that the way God deals with humankind *was* a bit of a mystery for a long time—the truth kept within the people of Israel, and hidden for the finding in the words and stories of the Old Testament. But now it is a mystery no longer. The gospel is a mystery where there is no longer any mystery! And it all centres on the person of Jesus Christ.

Christ—an open secret

Read Colossians 1:15-20

> ❷ *What has been revealed in Christ, according to Paul?*
> ❷ *What mysteries about God remain if we are able to encounter Christ therefore?*

Paul's language here is all about revelation. Christ reveals the true nature of God. And Christ becomes the means of redemption for his people, the church. The gospel—and the first of our seven words is his name and title "Christ", because Christ's identity, person and work *is* the good news we proclaim. This is reinforced by the first three words of verse 28. "*Him* we proclaim..." We are not promoting a scheme or a principle or a system. We are proclaiming a person.

☑ Apply

So when the opportunity arises to talk about what you believe, where do you start, and what is your focus? Of course there are many great things we can say about church, or the doctrines of grace or apologetically about how Christianity makes sense of ourselves or the world. But the true gospel must always centre on Christ himself.

☒ Pray

Lord, help me to openly proclaim Christ today by the way I live and the words I speak.

Bible in a year: 2 Chronicles 34-36 • Luke 11:29-54

Christ

We saw yesterday that Christ's person and identity is at the heart of the gospel. Today we see how his work completes the picture.

Christ's work
Read Colossians 1:18-22

❓ *What big word pictures does Paul use to describe what Jesus achieved for us?*
❓ *How did he do it (v 20-21, see also v 18)?*
❓ *What strikes you as strange about what Paul says here?*

The apostle moves effortlessly between big universal spiritual ideas—peace, reconciliation, purification, justification—and the brutal physicality of how Christ achieved them for us: a bloody death, torn and drained of life on a wooden cross. He says we are reconciled "by Christ's *physical* body" to emphasise both the historicity of Jesus' life, death and resurrection, and to show that redemption is for our own physical selves, not just some vague transaction in the spirit world. Again we can see how Paul is showing the distinctive difference between the gospel message and the religions of the day. These were based on mythic stories, and promised spiritual renewal in a way that despised or rejected our physical bodies as intrinsically evil, or irrelevant.

⌄ Apply

❓ *How would you explain each of the pictures of Christ's work to someone unfamiliar with the Christian message?*
• *Making peace (v 20)*
• *Reconciliation (v 22)*
• *Purification ("presents you holy", v 22)*
• *Justification ("free from accusation")*
❓ *Which of these pictures do you think has most relevance to the people you know?*

Christ...
Read Colossians 1:27

❓ *What do you understand by the name "Christ" and why is that important for the gospel message?*

Christ is the Greek word for the Hebrew term "Messiah"—and simply means "the anointed king". For Christians it is a word filled with significance. Jesus is the promised Messiah—the coming King—from the Old Testament. He is the Son of David, who is himself a "christ", an anointed king. Jesus is God's chosen King, not just of the church but of the entire cosmos (v 18). This is the Christ that we proclaim: King and Saviour.

⌄ Apply

An easy way to explain the gospel is by using the name Jesus Christ. "Christ" tells us who he is; Jesus (= rescuer) tells us why he came and what he did. Why not practise explaining that with another believer today?

⌃ Pray

Lord Jesus, thank you that you bled, died and rose again to rescue me. Help me share this good news with someone else today.

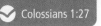

In you

There are Guinness world records for the greatest number of people you can fit in a telephone box or a Mini.* But this is a far greater challenge…

Where is Jesus?
Read Colossians 1:15-22

❓ *What words and phrases does Paul use to show how great and glorious Jesus Christ is?*

❓ *What do these verses suggest is the answer to the question "Where is Jesus"?*

❓ *What portrait do these verses paint of the situation of human beings in relation to God?*

Christ is the supreme Ruler, the Creator, the "glue" that holds the universe together. Without him, everything would fall apart (v 17). The fullness of God's character and nature is poured into his glorious Son. By contrast, we are at war with God—alienated from him and enemies in our thinking. Evil in our behaviour; we are unholy, blemished, and stand both accused and guilty before him as Judge.

Where is Jesus?
Read Colossians 1:27

❓ *Why is this statement such a shock?*

❓ *How do you understand what it means for Christ to be "in you"?*

It is indeed a staggering claim. This Christ—who is the very image of God—is in you. The one whose word stills storms, banishes sickness, causes demons to flee is *in you*. The one whose wisdom and teaching silenced the critics, challenged the compla-cent, and brought hope and joy to billions is *in you*. The one by whom the cosmos was created is *in you*. The one who made peace with you when you were evil, estranged and filled to the brim with sin is *in you*.

⌃ Pray

Pause to think about that for a moment, and turn your sense of wonder into gratitude and praise.

⌄ Apply

You can answer the question *where is Jesus?* in a number of ways. He is, of course, in heaven, seated at the right hand of the Father, as many Christians say in the creed week by week. He is also in all things—sustaining the universe by his powerful word. But, if you are a believer, he has also taken up residence in a special way in your life, in the person of the Holy Spirit—who directs all the glory and attention to the Lord Jesus Christ.

❓ *How does this truth encourage you to think differently about Christ and yourself?*

⌃ Pray

Lord Jesus Christ, thank you that you chose to make your home in me. Help me to make it a home worthy of you.

Bible in a year: Esther 3-5 • Luke 12:32-59

*The answer is 14 and 27 in case you were interested.

Christ in you—take 2

One way that the English language has fooled us is that the word "you" is both singular and plural. That distinction is hugely important in understanding the gospel message…

....

You or y'all?
Read Colossians 1:18-22

Wherever you read "you" in this passage, you need to understand that it is plural, not singular. If we were in the American South, the word would be best translated "y'all" (plural) not "you" (singular).

> ❓ *How does this change the way you think about these verses?*
> ❓ *How does it tie in with verse 18?*
> ❓ *What are we in danger of doing if we think that the "you" is singular? Where does this false thinking lead?*

Colossians is written to a whole church congregation—not just to an individual. Of course, the gospel promise is to individuals. But it is to individuals to come and be part of a group of people who he is saving as a whole. If you are a believer, Jesus has saved you. But he has saved you as part of the whole church. Jesus died for you, yes. But he died for you because he died for his people as a whole.

Forgetting this means we can have a very individualistic faith. It is all about Jesus and me, and other Christians can be relegated to the status of optional extras. But when we truly embrace it, we start to see that we are intimately and eternally bound together with other Christian believers from all over the globe. We are the same tribe and race and priesthood bound to each other by the blood and indwelling of his Spirit. We belong to one another. And this is the truth that should find expression every time we meet together.

Christ in us
Read Colossians 1:27

> ❓ *How does this perspective change the way you think about "Christ in you"?*
> ❓ *How does it change the way you think about why and how you gather together as Christian believers?*

⌄ Apply

Being part of a church can never be an optional extra. It is an essential part of who and what we are as believers in Christ. It is why unity among God's people is so important. It is why Communion—the breaking of bread—is so precious to us. It is why falling out of the habit of meeting together is so disastrous for our spiritual lives.

> ❓ *Have you wandered away from this priority? What will you do about it?*

⌃ Pray

Lord Jesus Christ, thank you that you have called me to belong to the glorious gathering of those you are bringing with you to the new creation. Help me to rejoice with and for my brothers and sisters in Christ today.

The hope

Covid-19, war and now economic uncertainty. Life has been so difficult, so challenging, so upsetting in recent years. We could all do with a bit of hope…

Vague hope

❓ *How do people use the word "hope" in ordinary life?*

Often people mistake optimism for hope. That vague feeling or attitude that "everything will turn out all right". And there is a sense in which active optimism can be self-fulfilling. If you work hard, you get lucky and things are much more likely to improve. But if you lack that positive spirit about the future, it leads to inactivity, and any possibility of things improving remain unborn. This is the kind of hope that self-help gurus peddle—often with a dash of fake spirituality ladled on top.

Sure hope

Read 1 Peter 1:3-4

❓ *What is distinctive about the way the Bible uses the word "hope"?*
❓ *What is this hope based on?*
❓ *What is this hope focused on?*

This is not vague, wishful-thinking hope. It is the "living hope" that the gospel talks about and promises. Gospel hope is a present confidence about a sure future that is based on the evidence of the past. Peter says that it is the fact of Jesus' resurrection from the dead that, often against the evidence of our current experience, enables us to stick confidently to the hope that we will one day be raised with him for all eternity. This is

the hope that enables people to endure suffering that would crush anyone else. This is the hope that drives people to travel the world and share the gospel at the peril of their own lives. This is the living hope that keeps Christians faithful in their witness to hostile or disinterested family and friends for decades. It is hope based on who God is and what he has done, rather than on ourselves.

⌄ Apply

❓ *Would you say that you are experiencing this kind of "living hope" day by day?*
❓ *When this hope fades in you, which it does in many from time to time, what do you think the remedy might be?*
❓ *How does it help to know that this is a hope you share with other Christians as you meet together week by week?*

⌃ Pray

If you are feeling weary and a bit hopeless after the battering we have all had these past few years, reflect on these words: "But those who hope in the LORD will renew their strength. They will soar on wings like eagles; they will run and not grow weary, they will walk and not be faint." Isaiah 40:31.

Lord thank you for the sure hope we have in Christ. I pray that this hope would bring life and vitality to my heart and soul today.

 Bible in a year: Esther 9-10 • Luke 13:22-35

Of glory

We saw yesterday what hope is and what it is based on for a Christian believer. Today we're looking at the object of our hope: glory!

Most people set themselves a series of goals in life. Raise a family. Own a house. Get promoted at work. Or more often, to enjoy good holidays, find a partner or eat well. These are not the ultimate goals for a Christian.

This world is not my home

Read Colossians 1:27

❷ *What do you understand by the term "glory"?*

❷ *Why do you think Paul calls it this, rather than another more common term?*

❷ *What picture comes into your mind when you think about "glory"?*

Whatever you picture when you think about heaven, the new creation or eternity, Paul wants us to focus on its essential quality, rather than on the details of what it will be like—most of which are unknown to us.

- **It will be glorious.** The pictures of the new creation we get in Scripture channel a sense of peace, plenty and astonishing wealth and beauty.

- **We will be glorious.** People who are alienated, wrong-thinking, evil, blemished and guilty (v 21-23) are still amazing and wonderful. Just imagine what the redeemed will be like when our true selves are finally revealed in the new creation!

- **Jesus will be glorious.** At the heart of the new creation described in Revelation will be the one who made it possible for us to be there, shining like the sun. We will see the Son of Man in all his splendour, and worship him gladly, freely and passionately.

···· **TIME OUT** ·······································

If you'd like a foretaste of the glory we will experience, **read Revelation 22:1-5** with a smile on your face, and a tear of joy in your eyes.

▾ Apply

We are on a journey together from a lost world to a glorious future. "This world is not my home, I'm just a-passing through, my treasures are laid up somewhere beyond the blue" as the old song goes.

❷ *Do you live as if that is true, or are you so concerned with earthly goals that the hope of glory has taken second place?*

❷ *Read the whole seven-word phrase again and mull over each word. Is this the gospel that you have embraced? Is it the gospel that you rejoice in and want to share with others?*

▲ Pray

Father, thank you that your glorious Son lives in me, and in all who have put their trust in him. Help me to be established and firm in this faith and to cling to the hope of the gospel until I reach glory.

My God is bigger

I work with someone who is tall, really tall—6ft 7in tall. He is a gentle giant, but I would feel much safer walking through a difficult neighbourhood if I were with him.

This psalm reminds us that when we trust in God, we trust in someone bigger than any problem we could face.

Out of the frying pan
Read 1 Samuel 21:10-15

David has fled Israel, where King Saul wants him dead, and sought refuge in Gath. Given that Gath's most famous son was Goliath (17:4), it's not surprising that things don't turn out so well when the inhabitants realise who David is. If you have time, turn to Psalm 34 to see how David praised God when he escaped...

On the run
Read Psalm 56:1-7

❷ *What are the different dangers that David is facing in these verses?*
❷ *Can you think of ways that these verses are fulfilled in the life of Jesus?*

God sees, knows, cares
Read Psalm 56:8-13

God may be running a universe, but verse 8 shows that he cares intimately for each one of us. No child of God ever shed an unseen tear.

It's important to remember David's encounter with Goliath some years earlier. The Israelite soldiers were all quaking in their sandals because Goliath was literally twice the size of them. But David made a different comparison. He did not compare himself to the giant, but the giant to God: "Who is this uncircumcised Philistine that he should defy the armies of the living God?" (1 Samuel 17:26). Now in Goliath's home town, David fights fear the same way.

❷ *What comparison does he make in Psalm 56:4 and 10-11?*
❷ *How confident is David that God will do as he has promised and deliver him?*

▾ Apply

❷ *When are you tempted to give in to fear of man, rather than to trust in God?*
❷ *What problems or anxieties are you facing at the moment?*
❷ *What determines whether you feel confident and calm to face them, or overwhelmed and sleepless with anxiety?*

▴ Pray

Take time to think about where in the Bible you see God deal with situations like that.

Now pray for the things that worry you and for those you love, in the light of verses 4 and 10-11.

Bible in a year: Joshua 1-3 • Luke 14:25-35

AARON'S BLESSING

Leaders often say it at the end of a church service; churches sang it during the pandemic—but what does this blessing actually mean for us now?

We're going to spend the week digging deep into this prayerful blessing to work that out.

Read Numbers 6:22-27

What?

"We wish you a merry Christmas and a happy New Year" it says in cards and texts we send and receive at this time of year. But it's worth thinking about what precisely is going on as we say, send and read these words...

> ❷ *What does it actually mean to "wish" such things for someone? How much power do such wishes have to bring about what you wish for?*
> ❷ *How does verse 27 make clear that this biblical blessing is different?*
> ❷ *How should that encourage us to use it?*

Who?

> ❷ *Who was to say this blessing (v 23)?*
> ❷ *What was special about them?*
> ❷ *To whom was the blessing to be said (v 23, 27)?*
> ❷ *In light of this, how do you think we should use it today?*

In the New Testament the priest in the first place is Jesus—so it is the Lord who speaks this blessing today. But those who are in Christ are also priests, so we can say it as well. It's not wrong for a church leader to say it at the end of a service, but he's no

more a priest than any other Christian. And the blessing is for God's people. It's not an assurance that God will bless non-Christians just because these words have been said or sung to them.

How?

> ❷ *Does anything strike you about how the blessing is structured (v 24-26)?*

The word "Lord" is repeated at the beginning of each line. He, the generous, covenant-making God, who is committed to his people, is the source of every blessing, so we need to look to him.

There are six things he is being asked to do, arranged in three pairs. The blessing is laid out in three lines, with each longer than the previous one—3, 5 and then 7 words in the original. The structure gives the impression of a stream of blessing that gets ever stronger. And this blessing is for *all* God's people—if we take out the word "Lord" we are left with 12 words in the original—the number of the tribes of Israel. But the "you" is singular. So this blessing is for each of us as individual believers.

🔺 Pray

Pray the words of this blessing for yourself and for other believers you know. Ask God to lead you into a deeper understanding of it in the coming days.

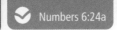

Bless you

When someone sneezes, people sometimes say "Bless you". But it's just being polite. The words have become meaningless in everyday life.

But actually the blessing of God upon us is what we need more than anything.

Read Numbers 6:22-27

Serious

Apparently, the tradition of saying "Bless you" when someone sneezes dates back to the 14th century, when the bubonic plague was ravaging Europe. One of the symptoms of this deadly disease was coughing or sneezing, so saying, "God bless you" was asking God to keep people from the Black Death. It was a serious thing—as is this prayer for blessing.

Read Matthew 25:34, 41

> ❓ *At the final judgment, what two categories of people will there be?*
> ❓ *And what contrasting eternal futures await them?*

Nothing matters more than making sure we are among the blessed rather than the cursed.

Gracious

By nature, as sinners, we all deserve to be cursed.

> ❓ *But what did God promise Abraham (see Genesis 12:1-3)?*

The whole Bible story is essentially about how we can get this blessing.

> ❓ *How has this promise to Abraham now been fulfilled (Galatians 3:7-14)?*

Through faith in Christ, we enjoy God's gracious blessing rather than the curse we deserve.

☑ Apply

As Christians we have been blessed in Christ, but we should pray for that blessing to continue, and for a deeper appreciation and experience of it; and for non-Christians to come to be blessed through faith in Christ.

Spiritual

Read Ephesians 1:3

> ❓ *What does this verse tell us about the blessings we have in Christ?*

In the Old Testament God's blessing was often experienced in tangible, material ways—land, health, prosperity, children. In the New Testament the blessings God promises us in the gospel are spiritual. It's not wrong to pray for material blessing—health, work, money to live—and we should certainly give thanks for these things, but what he promises now is spiritual blessing.

⌃ Pray

Give thanks for how God has blessed you richly in Christ. Pray for ongoing blessing, and for a deeper grasp of it.

Bible in a year: Joshua 7-9 • Luke 15:11-32

Keep you

John Newton wrote in his famous hymn, "Tis grace has brought me safe thus far, and grace will lead me home". Being kept safe is what this next bit of the blessing is about.

Read Numbers 6:22-27

Preservation: God will keep you

To "keep" means to watch over, guard, protect, preserve.

Read Genesis 28:15

> ❷ *When Jacob fled from his brother, Esau, the Lord promised to keep him. What would that have involved?*

As we journey to the heavenly country and city, we face what Newton in his hymn calls "many dangers, toils and snares".

> ❷ *What are some examples of the spiritual threats and dangers we face?*

Our greatest need, facing such threats, is for the Lord to keep us. The "Songs of Ascents" (Psalms 120 – 134) are a collection of psalms for ancient pilgrims heading up to Jerusalem. The language of the Numbers 6 blessing often surfaces in them.

Read Psalm 121

> ❷ *What comfort does the psalm give us as we journey to the heavenly Jerusalem?*

🔺 Pray

Using the words of the psalm, give thanks that the Lord has kept you safe thus far—and pray he will continue to keep you and lead you home.

Perseverance: keep yourself

But the Lord keeping us does not mean we can be spiritually lazy and complacent.

> ❷ *To which generation of God's people was the blessing originally spoken (Numbers 1:1)?*
> ❷ *What happened to them (14:21-24)?*

The Egypt escapees would later perish in the wilderness because of their rebellion and disobedience. The Numbers blessing wasn't some magic spell which automatically kept them safe—and nor will it keep us safe if we harden our hearts, as they did.

Read Jude 21, 24

> ❷ *What do these verses say about our need to keep ourselves, as well as trusting the Lord to keep us?*

⌄ Apply

> ❷ *What "habits of grace" should we be cultivating to keep ourselves in the faith and in God's love?*
> ❷ *How can we watch out for fellow believers, and they for us?*

🔺 Pray

Pray that the Lord would keep you; and that you would be diligent in keeping yourself, and others.

Shine upon you

We all love a sunny day. The sun brings warmth and joy—and life. No sun, no life. But an even greater blessing than sunshine is to have God's face shining on us.

Read Numbers 6:22-27

Smiley face

A repeated request in the Old Testament by God's people is for the light of God's face to shine on them.

Read Psalm 31:16; 67:1; 80:3, 7, 19

This is what we desperately need—to enjoy the light of God's favour. Even if it's a grey, rainy day outside, if the light of God's face is shining on us, it's a sunny day in the sense that matters most.

Angry face

But the sunshine of God's face is not something we can take for granted.

Read 1 Peter 3:12

❓ *What does this verse tell us about God's face?*

Read Revelation 6:15-16

❓ *How do people react to God's face at the final judgment?*

God's angry face in judgment is his response as a holy God to sin. It is utterly terrifying, but is what we deserve.

Christ's face

But the sunshine of God's face has now been revealed in the person of Jesus Christ.

At his transfiguration we read that "his face shone like the sun" (Matthew 17:2), and in John's vision of the risen, exalted Christ (Revelation 1:16) "his face was like the sun shining in all its brilliance".

Read 2 Corinthians 4:6

❓ *What happens when God shines his light in our hearts through the gospel?*

Read Revelation 22:4

❓ *If we trust in Christ, what can we look forward to?*

Fanny Crosby wrote over 8000 hymns. She was blind for most of her life, after being given wrong treatment as a 6-week-old baby by a fake doctor. But she later said, "When I get to heaven, the first face that shall ever gladden my sight will be that of my Saviour".

🔼 Pray

Give thanks...

- that through faith in Christ we enjoy the light of God's face shining on us.
- for the sure hope that one day we will see his face.

Pray for those you know who are currently heading for a terrifying encounter with God's angry face in judgment—that through Christ they would come to experience sunshine instead.

Be gracious to you

The Lord's shining face and amazing grace go together. Because of our sin, his face can only shine upon us if he is gracious to us.

Read Numbers 6:22-27

Gracious God

We cannot see God, and so if he hadn't revealed himself to us, we wouldn't have any idea what he is like. But thankfully he has revealed himself, not just in the glory of creation but in words.

Read Exodus 33:18-20; 34:6

❷ *What did God tell Moses about his character? How is that different to what some people might think God is like?*

❷ *How would you explain to someone the difference between grace and mercy?*

God is a gracious God. If mercy is not giving us the judgment we *do* deserve, grace is giving us the forgiveness and life which we *don't* deserve. Grace is a gift.

🔼 Pray

Give thanks that the gracious God shines the light of his face on people like us who don't deserve it.

Grace in Christ

The gracious character of God, revealed to Moses, finds its ultimate expression in "the gospel of God's grace" (Acts 20:24).

❷ *What do the following verses tell us about God's grace?*

• *John 1:14-18; Romans 3:23-25; Ephesians 2:8-9; Titus 2:11*

🔽 Apply

In our worst moments we can feel that God owes us, and that the blessings we enjoy are ours by right. He doesn't, and they aren't. What God owes us is judgment. Every good thing we have is a gift. Give thanks for his amazing grace to you in Christ.

Grace today
Read Luke 18:9-14

If we don't hold on tightly to God's grace in Christ, we will drift into the self-righteousness of the Pharisee in this story.

❷ *How did his self-righteousness shape how he viewed himself and other people (v 9, 11-12)?*

❷ *How did it affect his relationship with God (v 14)?*

🔽 Apply

Self-righteousness is very ugly. God hates it. But, if we're honest, we may at times see something of the Pharisee rather than the tax collector in our own heart and behaviour. Confess that to God now; make "Lord be gracious to me" your daily prayer; and give thanks for the gospel of God's grace.

Turn his face towards you

The atheist Richard Dawkins says that the universe has "no design, no purpose, no evil, no good, nothing but pitiless indifference".

Nothing could be further from the truth, as this blessing in Numbers reveals.

Read Numbers 6:22-27

May he turn his face

Our focus today is on the phrase "the LORD turn his face towards you". It means that he pays attention to us and is committed to our good.

> ❓ *Why is it an extraordinary thing that God should turn his face towards you or me?*

⌃ Pray

Give thanks that the universe is not as Dawkins imagines it; rather, that God is there, and the Creator and Ruler of everything pays attention to you and me as his people, and is committed to our welfare.

He may hide his face

But the Bible also speaks about the Lord hiding his face from his people.

Read Psalm 13:1-6

> ❓ *Why did David feel that the Lord had hidden his face from him?*

Sometimes in life, when we're going through hard times, it can feel like God is hiding—although he isn't—and our prayers seem to go unanswered. At such times we

need to keep trusting, and not listen to our feelings. But at times God may actually be hiding his face...

Read Psalm 30:5-7

> ❓ *According to verse 5, why might the Lord at times hide his face from his people (see also Psalm 27:9 which makes the same connection)?*
> ❓ *How do you think it might feel to experience this when it happens?*

It's part of God's loving discipline of us, that when we go astray and sin against him, he is rightly angry at our sin and hides his face from us. He feels distant, and it's as if the sun has gone behind the clouds.

We must seek his face

Read Psalm 27:8

> ❓ *At such times, what do we need to do?*
> ❓ *What does this involve (2 Chronicles 7:14)?*

⌄ Apply

If God feels distant at the moment, it might be because of sin from which we need to turn. Ask God by his Spirit to reveal that to you, and come back to him now. Seek his face, and so experience the blessing again of the Lord turning his face towards you.

And give you peace

The three lines of the blessing get longer, as they build up to the grand finale—peace. This is the ultimate blessing.

Read Numbers 6:22-27

Grace and peace

The Hebrew word for peace—*shalom*—wasn't just the absence of war. It was the sum total of all God's good gifts to his people. It was life as it was created to be lived. This is ultimately what God wants for us.

- ❷ *What is the relationship between grace (v 25) and peace (v 26)?*
- ❷ *Almost all the New Testament letters (all except Hebrews, James, 1 John and 3 John) begin with a greeting about "grace and peace", echoing this blessing in Numbers. Why, do you think?*

⌃ Pray

Give thanks for the peace we enjoy through God's grace. And pray that "grace and peace [would] be yours in abundance"(1 Peter 1:2).

Three dimensions

The gospel is "good news of peace through Jesus Christ" (Acts 10:36).

Read Romans 5:1,10

- ❷ *What three different dimensions of peace do these verses reveal?*
- ❷ *Why do people desperately need this peace?*

During the global pandemic, in March 2020, 65 UK churches came together to sing the Numbers blessing over the country. The video went viral and has had some 5 million views to date. It's a great encouragement to Christians, but why might it be potentially misleading for non-Christians? One repeated phrase is "He is for you".

Read Philippians 4:6-7

- ❷ *What do we need to do to enjoy this kind of peace?*

Read Ephesians 2:14-18

- ❷ *How do we see this peace in the church?*

World at peace

Jesus warned that until the end of the age there would continue to be wars, with nation rising against nation (Matthew 24:6-7).

Read Isaiah 9:6-7; Zechariah 9:10

- ❷ *What will the future world be like when Jesus returns to rule?*

⌃ Pray

Give thanks that through faith in Christ we enjoy peace with God, peace in our hearts, and peace with others who are in him. And we can look forward to life in eternity with him and his people in a world at peace. Then we will enjoy the ultimate fulfilment of this blessing in Numbers. Until then, why not include this blessing in your daily prayers.

FOR GOD SO LOVED

John 3:16, the verse we are going to focus on this week before Christmas, deserves its place as the most well-known verse in the Bible. Why? Because it so neatly encapsulates the broad sweep of the gospel message. And it starts with God.

"For God so loved the world that he gave his one and only Son, that whoever believes in him shall not perish but have eternal life."

There is a God and he's not out to get you!

Read John 3:16-21

The evidence for God's existence is all around us. The very existence of the universe points us towards the grand architect whose power and skill brought it into being. The beauty of the natural world speaks of God's kindness. Our sense of morality tells us there is a higher judge and moral authority—that right and wrong really matter.

❓ *Which of the evidences for God's existence (creation or morality) do you find most compelling and why?*

When we speak of God's love we remember it isn't something God *has* or *does* but rather something he *is*. His love does not come and go as ours often can. It is constant and perfect. We need never fear that one day he'll fall out of love with his bride, the church. His love is seen in many ways including his care for flowers and birds, and his sovereign control of the weather (see Matthew 5:45 and Luke 12:22-28).

❓ *Do you ever stop to consider something as simple as a snowdrop as evidence of God's love?*

❓ *Do you feel you're just too busy to notice these evidences of his existence and kindness all around us? What can you do about that?*

God is not a harsh figure, watching you and waiting to catch you out, and then punish you. He is compassionate and tender. He loves all he has made. He particularly loves his children. And because his love is his very essence, he will never stop loving us.

···· **TIME OUT** ··

Read 1 John 1:5-7; 4:7-8

❓ *Why is it important for us to remember that God is both light and love?*

☑ Apply

❓ *What is the dominant image that comes into your mind when you think about God?*
❓ *How does that shape your relationship with him in both positive and negative ways?*

⌃ Pray

Thank God that his love welcomes believers to come to him as his children

Pray for someone you know who needs to know God loves them today

Pray for someone who doesn't know Jesus that they would come to know his love.

The world

God loves the world, but we need to be careful to ensure we understand that statement correctly.

....

"For God so loved the world that he gave his one and only Son, that whoever believes in him shall not perish but have eternal life."

Read John 3:16, 19-20

The "world" in John's writing does not refer to the cosmos or every human being. You can see this by quickly reading John 7:7; 17:14, 16. Being of the "world" is a bit like being Irish or French—it refers to a collective cultural identity which to some degree defines us. From God's perspective being "world-ish" is who we are.

❓ *What are some of the characteristics of those who are "of the world"?*

Being of "the world" in John's writing refers to our natural sinfulness in rebelling against our Creator. And it's not just about my individual life. Sinful humans interact with other sinful humans creating whole cultures which live out rebellion against God. In a secular culture indifference towards God will look the right and normal thing.

❓ *How do you see human sinfulness building a sinful culture in your country or area?*

All of this makes John's claim even more remarkable—God sent his Son to and for the rebels, not the righteous! We tend to think God's love extends to "good" or religious people. Yet John says God sent his Son for

people who know they aren't right before a holy God and need his forgiveness.

🔼 Pray

Take some time now to simply praise God that he sent his Son for us while we were so far away from him.

🔽 Apply

❓ *In what ways do you find it easiest to conform to the patterns of this world?*

🔼 Pray

Pray that God would help you to live in the world and love the world, without being of the world.

Pray for that person you know who seems most set against God, that God's love would overcome their hardness of heart.

And pray that many would discover that the Son who came at the first Christmas really is good news for the world of lost souls.

That he gave

At the very heart of the Christian faith is a gift from God.

....

"For God so loved the world that he gave his one and only Son, that whoever believes in him shall not perish but have eternal life."

Read John 3:16 and Ephesians 2:8-9

The gospel is a gift. It is not won or earned by our own effort or brilliance. God's gift is pure grace. He did everything necessary to offer us salvation as a free gift. Of course in one sense it is not free. It cost him a great deal as we shall see, but that means it can be free to us, if we accept it. In the ancient world this was a strange idea. All gifts came with strings attached. Any gift was accompanied with the expectation of something in return. Not so with God's gift. He gives the gift of salvation to his children for no other reason than he loves them.

> ❓ *Can you think of a time when you received a gift that came with strings attached. How did it make you feel?*

If we reject grace and start to think of ourselves earning God's favour through our works we end up in one of three desperate places.

- First, we may try, fail, and be left feeling worthless.
- Second, you may try, fall short and feel resentment towards God.
- Third, you may actually think you've hit the mark, and then think God is somehow in your debt.

Each of these ways of thinking about a relationship with God are toxic and rob us of the joy of knowing his undeserved love.

> ❓ *Do you feel that your service at church, sharing the gospel with others, or even reading the Bible daily with Explore, is a duty and a chore?*
> ❓ *How should grace, rather than works, shape how you think about your own obedience to Christ?*
> ❓ *How can you encourage yourself and others to think in this way?*

⌄ Apply

> ❓ *Grace protects us from both pride and despair. Which of these two are you most tempted towards?*
> ❓ *What would a life of gratitude as a response to grace look like?*
> ❓ *Where might this be missing in your own life?*

⌃ Pray

Listen to or read (or sing!) the lyrics of that great hymn, "Amazing Grace", and spend some time meditating on the words and praising God for his grace.

Pray that his grace may ignite a greater response of gratitude in your own walk with him.

 Bible in a year: Nehemiah 7-9 • Luke 20:1-26

His one and only Son

God could not give just any gift—there was only one that would accomplish his purposes.

"For God so loved the world that he gave his one and only Son, that whoever believes in him shall not perish but have eternal life."

Readers of a certain age will recall Chesney Hawkes singing, "I Am the One and Only", a claim which, in retrospect, seems faintly ridiculous. However, on the lips of Jesus Christ the claim is both right and necessary!

❓ *Have you ever stopped to think about why God had to send his Son to our world?*

Read John 3:16 and Hebrews 10:11-14

Of all the gifts God lavishes on his creatures it is only Christ that could deal with the biggest breakdown between us and God—*our sin*. Because Jesus is human he could pay for our sin where the blood of bulls and goats never really could. Because Jesus is divine his blood is of infinite worth and can therefore pay for the sins of all his followers. Only God the Son could live the perfect life and die the atoning death in our place. The gift came at great cost to himself, and yet it is offered to us freely. We will never get over the astonishing wonder of such a gift.

The earliest Christians saw that bad maths made for good theology. The boy from Bethlehem had to be both 100% man and 100% God, not 50% man and 50% God.

❓ *Why is it so important to maintain that Jesus is both fully God and fully man?*

☑ Apply

❓ *What does this teach us about other religions or paths to God?*
❓ *What does the value of this gift tell you about your worth to God?*

⌃ Pray

Pray for someone you know who is seeking salvation through another religious path. Pray that they would see God the Son and all he brings.

Spend some time simply praising God for his incredible kindness in giving his Son, Jesus, to die that you might be his for eternity.

That whoever believes

Is it possible that the gift of God could be for absolutely anybody?

"For God so loved the world that he gave his one and only Son, that whoever believes in him shall not perish but have eternal life."

❷ *If someone asked you to define "faith" what would you say?*

Read John 3:16-21; Hebrews 11:1 – 12:3

I don't like heights. I once had to do an abseil on a camp I was helping with. I knew in my head it was safe, but the churning in my stomach said otherwise. I had to get my feelings to submit to what I knew I could trust.

Faith is not about feelings or the absence of any questions, doubts or struggles. Faith is a simple trust in someone or something to deliver what they say. Every time I sit on a chair I exercise faith it will do its job. When I visit the doctor I exercise faith they will diagnose and treat me well. When I leave my car with a mechanic I exercise faith that they will fix my car. When I drop my parcel off at the post office I'm exercising faith that it will get to its destination. Faith is not a mystical feeling. It is trusting that what Jesus promised, he can deliver. Robert Murray McCheyne once said, "For every look at self, take ten looks at Christ". That's faith.

❷ *What practical things could you do to keep reminding yourself of God's promises?*

Notice too that the gift is for *anyone* who believes. It isn't for the really good or earnest people. It is for "whoever" believes.

This is a crucial reminder that we are saved not by works, but by faith. It is a trust based entirely on what Jesus has done for me, and not what I have done for him. Because it is based on his work, and not mine, it can be offered to absolutely anybody.

❷ *Do you think the gift of salvation could be offered to someone like Vladimir Putin? Why or why not?*

(Note: this question gets to the heart of whether you *really* understand grace.)

⌄ Apply

❷ *Think about whether your trust in Christ is based on his work or yours? What would those closest to you say?*
❷ *When we consider how freely God has extended grace to us, are we similarly extending grace to others?*
❷ *Is there anyone you are withholding grace from at the moment?*

⌃ Pray

Talk to God about your struggles, fears and doubts—this in itself is an exercise of faith that he can help you in these things.

If you don't feel strong in faith at the moment spend time thanking Jesus for all he's done for you, and then ask him to help you feel it more.

Shall not perish

While it is hard to believe, God's judgment is actually good news.

"For God so loved the world that he gave his one and only Son, that whoever believes in him shall not perish but have eternal life."

Read John 3:16-21, 35-36

God's judgment is difficult to think about. The idea that some of those closest to us— who we may be sharing Christmas dinner with tomorrow— may be facing God's just judgment makes many of us feel real distress. Often we simply choose not to think about it. It's just too painful. We wonder how a good and loving God can leave people to perish.

Pray

Stop now to bring before God our loved ones who still seem so far from him.

A good and just God

Although we often struggle emotionally with the idea of God's judgment, we must battle to remind ourselves that God is just and justice is good. God's judgment means that no evil will ruin his new creation. All evil will be dealt with. The biggest challenge for us is that evil is not something "over there" but rather something "in here"—in each and every human heart. We need Jesus to deal with the penalty, power and presence of this evil, our sin. All of us must make the choice: will we let Jesus pay for our evil or will we pay for it ourselves?

❷ Consider the ways in which God's just judgment is good news for a broken world.

Warnings are acts of love. If I saw you about to step in front of a bus and I yelled a warning you wouldn't think me unkind. In fact you'd think it wicked of me not to warn you. The warnings of Scripture are the loving words of a Father who longs for us to turn back to him before it is too late. We need to share these words with those who haven't heard, or perhaps don't want to hear.

❷ Think about the various ways in which warnings serve to protect and care—can you think of other examples?

···· TIME OUT ·······································

When it comes to sharing our faith we are often more concerned about people's opinion of us, than their eternal fate.

❷ How might we overcome our fear of other people?

Pray

Thank God that he gave his Son so that we need not fear judgment.

Pray for those you know who face eternity without him.

Ask God to give you courage to share your faith with someone close to you.

But have eternal life

Happy Christmas! Eternal life has nothing to do with pudgy babies, halos, harps and sitting on clouds. It is the reason we celebrate today as we do.

"For God so loved the world that he gave his one and only Son, that whoever believes in him shall not perish but have eternal life."

> ❷ *When you think of eternal life what kind of images come into your mind?*

Read: John 3:16-17; Revelation 21:1-4

When we think of heaven our minds are often drawn to cream-cheese adverts or medieval paintings. The Bible has a much better picture! Eternal life will be the glorious fulfilment of all that it means to be a creature. We will experience no more sorrow, mourning and pain. We will know a new depth of joy. The greatest gift of the new creation is being with God himself. All that we have known in part we will know in full.

> ❷ *What are you looking forward to most about eternal life? Have you ever pondered what it will feel like to meet Jesus face-to-face?*

And it will never end. There is no threat of being thrown out at closing time. Our joy will be unending, and it will never be boring! If you can imagine the moments of greatest happiness you've known, multiply them by a billion, then string them all together in unending succession, you're still not close to what eternal life with God will be like. We will discover that each new chapter is better than the previous one. And it is all secured and guaranteed for us by Jesus. This gives us a sure and certain hope,

not based on our performance, but entirely based on his. This is good news of great joy.

> ❷ *How does this vision of eternal life motivate you to live for Jesus in the here and now?*

✔ Apply

> ❷ *How does eternal life reframe the way we think about the "stuff" of this life?*
> ❷ *How does eternal life reframe the way we think about current pain and sorrow?*

^ Pray

Spend time praising Jesus because he's made a place for us and is waiting to welcome us in (see John 14:1-4).

Jesus often referred to eternity as a party—a glorious wedding feast. Pray that as you celebrate with church, family and friends today, you would look towards the eternal celebration in God's new creation.

KNOWING CHRIST

Philippians 3:9-10 are precious verses to me because they've helped me make sense of the ups and downs of life, and helped me face suffering and sacrifice with confidence.

We'll unpack them over this coming week as we prepare for a new year.

Paul writes that he wants to be "found in him, not having a righteousness of my own that comes from the law, but that which is through faith in Christ—the righteousness that comes from God on the basis of faith. I want to know Christ—yes, to know the power of his resurrection and participation in his sufferings, becoming like him in his death." Today we see how these verses help us face our guilt with confidence.

"I want to know Christ," says Paul in verse 10. It's the climax of a train of thought that starts in verse 1. Paul wants to know Christ because in Christ we find righteousness = being right with God.

Not from the law…

Read Philippians 3:1-8

❷ *What are the two commands here?*
❷ *How does Paul evaluate his own law-based righteousness?*

The first command is: "Rejoice" (v 1). The second is "watch out" (v 2). Don't be misled by people who tell you what to do to be a good Christian. Paul calls them "evildoers"— even though they advocate obeying God's law! Why? Because they're using God's law for the wrong purpose—to make themselves look good. The two commands go together. As soon as someone persuades you there's

something you must do to win God's approval, you've started to assume you don't already have it. What they advocate may be a good thing (like keeping God's law), but you're now thinking that God frowns upon you.

And here's the problem: you can never measure up through your own efforts. Paul's record was second to none (v 4-6). Yet what's his verdict? "Loss" and "garbage" (v 7-8). The religious works he once thought were in the credit column were actually in the loss column. They might have looked good, but they were a garbage heap of pride and self-reliance. They were just another way of rejecting God.

… but from God

Read Philippians 3:9-11

Why does Paul want to know Christ? Because in Christ we get true righteousness—the rightness of Christ with God given to us through faith. If you have faith in Christ then God the Father looks on you and thinks, *What a wonderful Christian.* He delights to hear you pray and see you serve. He delights in you. So rejoice in the Lord!

✔ Apply

- **Rejoice**: delight in God's delight in you.
- **Watch out:** when do you start thinking you need to prove you're a good Christian?

Bible in a year: Micah 6-7 • Luke 22:21-46

Christ my treasure

What's your motivation for obeying God? Why tell people about Jesus? Why give up your time to go to a prayer meeting? Why refrain from sex outside of marriage?

Enjoy yourself!

Read Philippians 3:1

- *Why might we find a command like this difficult to obey?*

In effect Paul says: *I know you've heard me say this before, but I need to say it again.* That might seem a bit odd. Why must Paul keep telling people to enjoy themselves? The answer is that human beings keep looking for joy in the wrong places. We don't look for joy "in the Lord".

Read Philippians 3:7-10

- *What's driving Paul's behaviour in these verses? What's his motivation?*

"For the sake of Christ." "The surpassing worth of knowing Christ." "That I may gain Christ." "I want to know Christ." Why is Paul willing to give up everything? Because Christ is worth it.

Happy in hardship

Read Philippians 1:12-18

- *Why can Paul rejoice even though he's in prison?*

Read Philippians 1:18-21

- *Why can Paul rejoice even though martyrdom is a real possibility?*

The great motivation of Paul's life is Christ. So he's happy because the gospel is advancing through his chains and he may have the opportunity to exalt Christ by his willingness to be martyred.

TIME OUT

Read Matthew 13:44-46

- *How does the message of these parables map onto Paul's testimony in Philippians 3?*

Apply

How would you complete the sentence, "For me, to live is..."? Sex? Money? Success? Pleasure? Reputation? Friendship? Career? Family? Christmas? Chocolate?

Sometimes these things bring us joy, but sometimes they don't. Only joy in Christ transcends every circumstance—even death. Death robs us of every other joy. But death means you get more of Christ rather than less of Christ. So when you can say, "For to me, to live is Christ" then you can say, "And to die is gain".

Imagine a pauper who marries a prince. All his wealth and honour become hers. But most of all she gets the love of her life.

When we are united to Christ we get his wealth and honour—his righteousness. But best of all we get Christ himself.

The power of Christ

Living as a Christian can feel like hard work. Giving in to temptation or giving way to fear can sometimes feel inevitable—so why resist?

But it's not true. We can experience resurrection power. "I want to know Christ," says Paul in Philippians 3:10, "yes, to know the power of his resurrection".

Power, strength, riches
Read Ephesians 1:15-21

❓ *What does Paul pray for in verses 18-19?*
❓ *How does he describe the power in Christians?*

The power that reached into the grave and raised Christ from the dead is the same power that reaches into our lives and raises us from spiritual death. If you are a believer, you have resurrection power pulsing through your veins. In Ephesians 1 Paul prays that the Ephesians will know this in their experience. In Philippians 3:10 he expresses his own desire to experience resurrection power.

Read Philippians 4:10-19

❓ *According to verses 13 and 19 what resources does God give to us?*
❓ *According to verses 11-12 what are we to use these resources for?*

Christ shares his strength with us! God meets our needs from "the riches of his glory". That's a store room that will never run dry. But it's not strength to indulge ourselves. It's strength to live a life that honours Christ. For Paul this included being content even when he was going hungry. It meant being content even when he was in chains or facing hardship.

☑ Apply

Some Christians talk a lot about power, but don't talk much about being content in any and every situation—especially when that includes ill-health or financial struggles. Other Christians talk a lot about being content in every situation, but don't talk much about resurrection power.

❓ *Which camp do you think you're in?*
❓ *Which camp is Paul in?*

Ordinary battles, extraordinary power

Christians are given resurrection power so we can win battles. Every now and then those battles are fought on a big stage—perhaps as people face martyrdom with fortitude. But for most of us, for most of the time, these battles are fought in the ordinary: the battle to be holy, to be selfless, to be faithful, to speak about Christ openly and unashamedly to others. The battlefield may be ordinary, but the power within us is extraordinary. It's the power of Christ and his resurrection.

❓ *What "ordinary battles" will you be facing today?*
❓ *How will you meet them today through him who gives you strength?*

Bible in a year: Zechariah 5-8 • Luke 23:1-25

The sufferings of Christ

We have rejoiced in the righteousness and power that are ours in Christ. But the Christian life is not plain sailing. And Paul recognises this fact.

Verse 10 continues: "I want to know Christ—yes, to know the power of his resurrection and participation in his sufferings". If we're linked to Christ then we can expect to suffer like Christ.

Read Philippians 1:27-30

> ❓ *What can Christians expect in the present according to these verses?*
> ❓ *What can Christians expect in the future according to these verses?*
> ❓ *How should we conduct ourselves in the meantime?*

We can expect to be opposed (v 28) and to suffer (v 29). In Christ we get righteousness and power. But suffering is also part of the package, at least in this life. After all, Christ was rejected by the world and we're now aligned to Christ. Jesus himself said, "If the world hates you, keep in mind that it hated me first" (John 15:18). This has certainly been Paul's own experience (Philippians 1:30).

☑ Apply

Even in the face of hostility, we are called to behave like Christ (27) and pull together (v 27) without giving in to fear (v 28). How can we do this? By remembering that, while our union with Christ may mean suffering now, it also means eternal salvation from God (v 28).

···· **TIME OUT** ····

Paul says he wants to participate in the

sufferings of Christ. *Really?* Is that right? Why would we welcome suffering? Moreover, this is part of an argument that begins with a call to "rejoice" (v 1). *Really?* How can we rejoice in suffering (3:10)?

Read 1 Peter 4:12-13; James 1:2-3

> ❓ *Why can we rejoice when we participate in Christ's sufferings?*

Power to endure

The power of resurrection and participation in suffering go hand in hand in the Christian life (as they do in Philippians 3:10). We need the power of the resurrection to follow the way of the cross. Self-denial and sacrificial love are not part of our natural instincts. But we have resurrection power, giving new desires and the strength to endure. Talking about power without talking about suffering is triumphalism; talking about suffering without talking about power is defeatism.

···· **TIME OUT** ····

Read 2 Corinthians 13:4; Colossians 1:10-11; 2 Timothy 1:7-8

> ❓ *In each case what have we been given power to do?*

☑ Apply

> ❓ *What have you suffered in the last year?*
> ❓ *What might you suffer in 2023?*
> ❓ *Are you able to rejoice in both?*

Shaped by Christ's death

Being united to Christ has changed the trajectory of our lives. It's as if we've hopped on board the Jesus-train and now we're heading off in a new direction.

The New Testament often describes Christians as those who are "in Christ". Think of Christ as a train and we're now sitting in one of the carriages. Now we're travelling both with Christ and in Christ. And our destination is glory. Christ will get us there—there's no doubt about that. But the route can take us down before it takes us up.

Read Philippians 2:5-11

> ❷ *What is the trajectory of Christ in verses 6-8?*
> ❷ *What is the trajectory of Christ in verses 9-11?*

Verse 5 is literally: "Have this mind among yourselves, which is yours in Christ Jesus" (ESV). In other words Paul is urging us to think of ourselves as those who are in Christ. One day that will mean up, up, up to glory—as it did for Jesus in verses 9-11. But first it means down, down, down to the cross—as it did for Jesus in verses 6-8.

A cross-shaped life

In the present our lives are to be shaped by the cross. Jesus himself said as much in his description of a disciple: "Whoever wants to be my disciple must deny themselves and take up their cross and follow me". (Mark 8:34) In Philippians 3:10 Paul talks about "becoming like [Christ] in his death". What does a life shaped by the cross look like? Self-denial, sacrificial love, service and suffering.

☑ Apply

Read Philippians 2:1-4

Philippians 2:5-11 is the rationale for the exhortations of Philippians 2:1-4.

> ❷ *What does a Christ-shaped life look like according to verses 1-4?*

Read Philippians 2:17-30

Paul gives three models of a Christ-shaped life: himself (v 17-18), Timothy (v 19-24) and Epaphroditus (v 25-30).

> ❷ *How do we see a Christ-shaped life being modelled in these three people?*

◢ Pray

Use Paul's prayer in Philippians 1:9-11 to shape your prayers today:

- To praise Christ for his sacrificial service.

- To pray for yourself—that you would follow in the footsteps of Christ in humble service.

- And to pray for others—that your fellow believers might display the love and glory of Christ in how they live in the world.

The glory of Christ

Being in Christ changes the trajectory of our lives. In the present that means a cross-shaped life of service. But the ultimate trajectory is up to resurrection glory.

A resurrection-shaped future

Philippians 3:10-11 says, "I want to know Christ ..." "becoming like him in his death, and so, somehow, attaining to the resurrection from the dead". In the present it is the cross that shapes our lives—albeit a cross-shaped life lived through resurrection power. But in the future the resurrection will shape our lives. Just as Christ experienced suffering followed by glory, those who are in Christ will experience suffering followed by glory.

···· **TIME OUT** ····································

Read Romans 8:17-18; 1 Peter 1:10-11; 4:12-13

❷ *What is the pattern for Christ?*
❷ *What is the pattern for those who are in Christ?*

Read Philippians 3:12-14

Paul is not there yet. His journey isn't over. You might expect Paul, being in prison, to leave the hard work of ministry to other people. Or you might expect Paul in old age to stop battling temptation. But Paul's not going to take his foot off the pedal until the journey is over. He's not reached the destination and so he presses on like someone running to win a prize.

☑ Apply

Twice Paul says "I press on" (v 12, 14).

❷ *What might it mean for you to press on in the year ahead?*
❷ *What might it look like if you were to stop pressing on?*

Somehow and surely

Paul says in verse 11, "... and so, somehow, attaining to the resurrection from the dead". That word "somehow" does not mean the end is in doubt. It's not that Paul is worried about whether he'll be raised. There's no doubt about resurrection glory because Christ is already there and we're in Christ. What's in doubt is the route. Paul's in prison and he doesn't know whether he's going to get out, stay in prison or be martyred (1:22-24). But one way or another the end is Christ—we can be sure of that.

We need to persevere if we're to make it to glory. But we press on confident that Christ will never let us go. "I press on to take hold of that for which Christ Jesus took hold of me." (3:12)

◣ Pray

Look back over the notes from the past few days and then turn each phrase of Philippians 3:10-11 into praise and prayer.

Introduce a friend to

explore

If you're enjoying using *Explore*, why not
introduce a friend? *Time with God* is our
introduction to daily Bible reading and is a
great way to get started with a regular time
with God. It includes 28 daily readings along
with articles, advice and practical tips on how
to apply what the passage teaches.

Why not order a copy for someone you
would like to encourage?

Coming up next...

- Judges
  with Nathan Buttery

- Luke 19 – 22
  with Carl Laferton

- Obadiah
  with Paul Jump and Anna Marsh

- Ecclesiastes
  *with John Onwuchekwa
  and Katy Morgan*

Don't miss your copy. Contact your local Christian
bookshop or church agent, or visit:

UK & Europe: thegoodbook.co.uk
info@thegoodbook.co.uk
Tel: 0333 123 0880
North America: thegoodbook.com
info@thegoodbook.com
Tel: 866 244 2165

Australia: thegoodbook.com.au
info@thegoodbook.com.au
Tel: (02) 9564 3555

India: thegoodbook.co.in
contact: @forthetruth.in
Tel: (+91) 8604685533

Truth for Life

A second volume of 365 Christ-centred daily devotions from renowned Bible teacher Alistair Begg. These concise devotions reflect on a few short verses each day for a year and are full of clear exposition and thoughtful application in Alistair's trademark warm, faithful and engaging style.

Reflecting on a short passage each day, Alistair spans the Scriptures to show us the greatness and grace of God, and to thrill our hearts to live as his children. His clear, faithful exposition and thoughtful application mean that this resource will both engage your mind and stir your heart.

thegoodbook.co.uk/truth-for-life
thegoodbook.com/truth-for-life